IMAGINE

IMAGINE

WHAT WOULD YOUR LIFE LOOK LIKE IF
YOU WERE TO BELIEVE EVERYTHING GOD
HAS SAID ABOUT YOU AND WRITTEN FOR
YOU?

Tim Shiels

Acknowledgements

To The Church,

Thank you for being the safest place in the world to fail forward. Thank you for being the safest place in the world to make mistakes. Thank you for bringing life, love and hope to the heart of my world. Don't Stop Believing.

To The Shiels Family,

In my darkest days you called me home. I wouldn't be here without you. Love and then love some more.

To James,

Thank you for covering my mistakes. This would not have happened without you. Keep Smiling.

To Darren,

Thank you for the inspiration. This would not have happened were it not for you. Keep Investing.

To Alan and Dorothy,

When I grow up I hope I can be like you. Thanks for allowing me to be part of your story. Keep going.

To Kristina,

Thanks for always adapting to change with endless grace

To you,

In writing this book, I have been transformed. In reading it I hope you are too. Imagine!

Please also know this

50% of the profit from the sale of this book will be used to make a significant difference in the lives of Jabulani Kids. Jabulani is a very special place due to the love, care and attention every child gets everyday. For more details on what they do, please visit jabukids.com

Introduction

I'm pretty sure that Imagine will not be the greatest book you've ever read. There are people in the world who are way more gifted at writing than I am.

I can promise you this, reading this book will encourage you, inspire you, and feed your soul.

It's a transformation story that goes from darkness to light.

The I AM statements included in each chapter have been the soundtrack to my life. I challenged myself to imagine what my life might look life if I dared to believe they were true. Somehow I've ended up here.

Be Blessed,

Tim

"Praise be to the God and Father of our Lord Jesus Christ, who has blessed us in the heavenly realms with every spiritual blessing in Christ. For he chose us in him before the creation of the world to be holy and blameless in his sight. In love he predestined us for adoption to sonship through Jesus Christ, in accordance with his pleasure and will— to the praise of his glorious grace, which he has freely given us in the One he loves. In him we have redemption through his blood, the forgiveness of sins, in accordance with the riches of God's grace that he lavished on us. With all wisdom and understanding, he made known to us the mystery of his will according to his good pleasure, which he purposed in Christ, to be put into effect when the times reach their fulfilment—to bring unity to all things in heaven and on earth under Christ. In him we were also chosen, having been predestined according to the plan of him who works out everything in conformity with the purpose of his will, in order that we, who were the first to put our hope in Christ, might be for the praise of his glory. And you also were included in Christ when you heard the message of truth, the gospel of your salvation. When you believed, you were marked in him with a seal, the promised Holy Spirit, who is a deposit guaranteeing our inheritance until the redemption of those who are God's possession—to the praise of his glory."
Ephesians 1:3-14 NIV

Table of Contents

CHAPTER ONE

I AM LOVED

Great love awaits those who believe they are loved…

"Dear friends, let us love one another, for love comes from God. Everyone who loves has been born of God and knows God." 1John 4:7 NIV

Life is full of defining moments. Moments that help shape us into who we become. The day you were born determines your age. The place you were born determines your nationality. Some moments arise, where our response can also determine our future. On 15th December 2019, during the Sunday service in Omagh Community Church, I stood up to preach. The church expected a dynamic sermon but I had nothing prepared. What the church didn't know was that 3 days earlier I was standing on a bridge, contemplating suicide. As I took to the platform, I was overcome with emotion. I was shaking, breathing heavily, and crying uncontrollably. I had nothing prepared and all I could say was I'm sorry that I have failed you and let you down as your pastor. I began to explain how scared, tired, weary and depressed I was feeling. As I was falling apart before them, the most beautiful thing happened. Alan Miller led the church in the most outrageously visible demonstration of grace and love I have ever witnessed in my life.

Alan has been a Pastor and leader in Omagh Community Church since its infancy and he and his wife are one of the godliest couples I have the privilege of knowing. As I was falling apart, Alan left his seat, walked toward me, put his arms around me, and held me in the most loving embrace.

What followed was nothing short of a miracle. One by one, people left their seats, walked to the front of the church, and surrounded me. As they surrounded me Alan began to pray. "Heavenly Father, we thank you that you sent Tim to be our Pastor. Heavenly Father, we thank you that you love Tim. Heavenly Father, we thank you that Tim loves us. Heavenly Father, we thank you that the schemes of the devil will not and have not prevailed. Heavenly Father, we thank you that you are building your church. Heavenly Father, we thank you that you died on the cross for Tim and that Tim has been raised to a new life in you." As Alan prayed, the church began to pray, the worship team began to play and we worshiped our way through one of the most defining moments of my life. I'm not sure if I can ever remember a time that I felt so loved.

I'm not sure if you've ever felt unloveable, but if you have, you'll no doubt understand the impact such a moment can have. In my darkest hour, love came down and touched my heart. It touched my heart in such a way that I will never be the same again. **Love is a wonderful thing, it changes everything it touches and it never fails.**

In his letter to the church in Rome, Paul writes, "You see, at just the right time, when we were still powerless, Christ died for the ungodly. Very rarely will anyone die for a righteous person, though for a good person, someone might dare to die? But God demonstrates his love for us in this: While we were still sinners, Christ died for us."
Romans 5:6-8

Paul reminds us that in our darkest hour when we are at our worst when we feel unlovable, we are loved by God. God wants us to know that his love never was, and never will be, dependent on our attitudes, actions, and behaviours, and although we can't earn it and certainly don't deserve it, it's ours and nothing we could ever say or do could ever take it away. We haven't done anything to deserve it and can't do anything to lose it.

Eugene Peterson translates Ephesians 1:3-6 like this "How blessed is God! And what a blessing he is! He's the Father of our Master, Jesus Christ, and takes us to the high places of blessing in him. Long before he laid down earth's foundations, he had us in mind and had settled on us as the focus of his love, to be made whole and holy by his love. Long, long ago he decided to adopt us into his family through Jesus Christ. (What pleasure he took in planning this!) He wanted us to enter into the celebration of his lavish gift-giving by the hand of his beloved Son." Ephesians 1:3-6 MSG

Most people equate love with emotion but I've come to understand that it is more than that. Love is an act of the will. Love is a choice. God has chosen us to be the object of his love and our acceptance of his love leads to the healthy transformation and restoration of our relationship with him, ourselves, and the world around us. Feeling loved is dependent on circumstance, but trusting that we are loved requires faith.

Many of us understand the concept of the holy trinity: Father, Son, and Holy Spirit. They co-exist and work together in unity to bring the plans and purposes of the Godhead to life. In our humanity, we also thrive when we operate within a trinity of relationships. For us to thrive and bring the plans and purposes of God to life, we need a healthy relationship with God, ourselves, and our neighbour, which is rooted and grounded in love. Paul writes in his letter to the Colossians that love binds us together in perfect unity. It's impossible to live the life made available to us through Jesus' life, death, and resurrection without loving God, yourself, and your neighbour. You cannot separate the three and thrive. The enemy of our soul knows this and will do everything he can to drive a wedge between them.

It's safe to say that 2019 wasn't what I would describe as a vintage year. On the 27th Feb, I boarded an airplane in Dublin and traveled to Copenhagen. As I stepped onto the plane I had no idea if I would ever return to my home or, if I did, what it would look like. My marriage was in tatters: Jennie and I had drifted so far apart that I didn't want to be a husband anymore. In addition to this, I was angry with God because I felt trapped in the relationship. After all, if I left my marriage, I would have to leave my church. Circumstances outside of my control had left me feeling angry, hurt, disappointed, frustrated, and miserable, and these feelings spilled into almost all my relationships.

Unity is hard to keep but it's always worth fighting for. It requires us to put on the full armour of God, to be filled with the Spirit of God, to love both ourselves and our neighbour, to make the needs of others a priority, to be patient, kind, generous, forgiving, polite, honouring, and humble.

The enemy's first attack on humanity came in the garden of Eden. He managed to find a way to make Adam and Eve doubt God's sovereignty and question God's words. He challenged their perception of God and their relationship with him. His influence drove a wedge between them and God which in turn impacted their relationship with themselves and each other. When they became aware of what had happened they felt shame and hid from God. That's what shame does, it causes us to hide. When God confronted them, they blamed each other, neither one wanting to accept responsibility for their actions. It always feels much easier to blame someone else than to accept responsibility for the mistakes we have made.

Satan's methods haven't changed since the beginning of time. He is still trying to make us think that we are separated from God, unloved and unloveable.

I allowed him to impact my world and influence my thinking in such a way that I believed I had become unloveable because I had failed and that God couldn't use a failure like me. My only option was to hide. I distanced myself from everyone, including God. I got as busy as possible to avoid accountability and ran myself into the ground.

The good news for us is that God's methods have also remained the same. He remains merciful, gracious, slow to anger, and abounding in steadfast love and faithfulness. The

New Testament teaches us that you cannot out-love God nor can you lose his love. The Old Testament teaches us that you cannot outrun God's love and that the steadfast love of God never fails. God is consistently and passionately pursuing his children and calling them home.

Everything changes when we know that we are loved. We find freedom. True freedom comes when we realise that we have nothing to hide. That's what love does. **Love allows us to expose the hidden areas of our lives, the deepest darkest crevices of our souls, our innermost secrets, without fear. It allows us to present our authentic broken selves without fear of rejection.** Love doesn't require us to be perfect, it only requires honesty and vulnerability. Love unites, love restores, and love builds up.

Everything changed on the day that I dared to believe that I am loved. I dared to believe that, amid past failures and present mistakes, God loves me. I dared to believe that even with all of my flaws my world loves me and loves the uniqueness of my personality. I found the freedom that only love can give when I dared to believe that I am loved.

These words, that God spoke through the prophet Jeremiah, paint a beautiful picture of the transformational power of God's love. They remind us of the continuous love, encouragement, and support made available by God to his children:

"The Lord appeared to us in the past, saying:I have loved you with everlasting love; I have drawn you with unfailing kindness. I will build you up again, and you, Virgin Israel, will be rebuilt. Again you will take up your timbrels and go out to dance with the joyful. Again you will plant vineyards on the hills of Samaria; the farmers will plant them and enjoy their fruit."
Jeremiah 31:3-6 NIV

The singer Whitney Houston would have you believe that loving yourself is the greatest love of all and that it's easy to achieve. I've learned that it is impossible to achieve without recognising and responding to the love of God. The love of God is a safe space that allows us to come as we are and wrestle with who we are becoming. The role God's love plays in each of our lives empowers us to love ourselves and love those around us.

When I realised that I was loved and loveable, I opened myself up to receive not only God's love but the love of those around me. It empowered me to stop hiding under a cloud of shame and allowed me to walk in the new freedom I had found.

His love changed my value system. I noticed my sleeping pattern improved, along with my eating and drinking habits. My responses changed and became gracious. I stopped looking and sounding angry. My countenance dramatically enhanced. I stopped looking and sounding miserable. I had the desire to exercise. I stopped avoiding church events. I became a social being, well, as social as an introvert can be. I had more patience with people, especially my family. What I watched on tv and listened to on the radio changed. I found joy. I had peace. I was gentler and kinder. I was reading. I got creative and began to imagine. I'm not suggesting that this happened overnight but as I continued to put on love every day and let the peace of God rule in my heart my life continued to change at a rapid rate.

Love is messy. It requires us to lay down our lives for the benefit of others. It requires sacrifice, the laying down of our expectations and agendas to see the fulfilment of God's plan in our own lives and the lives of those in our sphere of influence. Jesus modelled a love that works. He modelled the type of sacrificial love and service that leads to healing and transformation. He laid down his life so that we would know we are loved. He made us perfect and holy through his love. He empowers us to live loved through the work of his Holy Spirit. He challenges us to demonstrate our love for him through our love for those around us.

May God continue to bless those in my world who model this so well. May he continue to forgive me for the times that I don't.

In his first letter, the apostle John writes these words:
"Dear friends, let us love one another, for love comes from God. Everyone who loves has been born of God and knows God."
1John 4:7 NIV

He then goes on to say this:

"God is love. Whoever lives in love lives in God, and God in them. This is how love is made complete among us so that we will have confidence on the day of judgment: In this world, we are like Jesus. There is no fear in love. But perfect love drives out fear because fear has to do with punishment. The one who fears is not made perfect in love.

We love each other because he first loved us. Whoever claims to love God yet hates a brother or sister is a liar. For whoever does not love their brother and sister, whom they have seen, cannot love God, whom they have not seen. And he has given us this command: Anyone who loves God must also love their brother and sister."
1 John 4:16-21

Our ability to release God's love is directly proportional to our ability to receive God's love.

I don't claim to be a physics major. If anything I am most likely to describe myself as a physics novice whose knowledge is limited to what I can remember from my days at school. I do however remember what an electrical conductor is. A conductor, or electrical conductor, is a substance or material that allows electricity to flow through it. The same can be said of us as children of God, we are love conductors. God's love comes to us and flows through us in such a way that our lives and the lives of those around us are empowered to thrive. I can tell you without a shadow of a doubt that the one thing that is guaranteed to make me a better husband, father, friend, and son is God's love. I can also tell you without a shadow of a doubt that the one thing guaranteed to transform your relationships is the love of God.

God is the great provider. By putting his Spirit inside us, he has given us everything we need for life and godliness. His Spirit produces love in our lives and through our lives in such a way that we become great lovers.

Great love awaits those who believe that they are loved.

CHAPTER TWO

I AM A CHILD OF GOD

As children of God we are children of promise...

"Yet to all who did receive him, to those who believed in his name, he gave the right to become children of God". John 1:12

Let me tell you about the time I saw Jesus in Knock. Wikipedia describes Knock like this. "Knock is a village in County Mayo, Ireland. Its notability is derived from the Knock Shrine, an approved Catholic shrine, and place of pilgrimage where the faithful believe that the Blessed Virgin Mary, Saint Joseph, and Saint John the Evangelist appeared on 21 August 1879."

Knock is filled with shops that sell religious gifts and souvenirs. On one of our annual family trips, I was walking along with my sister and parents and I looked into a shop window. As I looked, I noticed the eyes of a picture following me as I moved. The picture itself was an image of Jesus with bright colours bursting out from his chest. No matter what angle I would look at the picture from, the eyes of the picture would follow me. In the heat of the moment and the excitement of the environment, I was utterly convinced that Jesus himself was making himself known to me. Jesus appeared to me in Knock. The blood drained from my face and I began to pray, much to the amusement of my family, I might add. The picture was a holographic image specially designed to move with its viewer. My parents knew that. My sister knew that. I didn't know that, and as a result, I was tricked into believing that Jesus had got my attention and was reaching out to me on a street in Knock. I still take great comfort in knowing that at that moment I had the faith to believe that Jesus in his divinity would be attempting to connect with me in my broken humanity.

There has never been a day in my life that I haven't believed in God. I have never had any difficulty in accepting the reality of a holy God. I have however had difficulty in accepting that a holy God would want to have a relationship with someone like me. For years, I found myself asking the question, "Why would God in his holiness want to have anything to do with someone as broken as me?". Maybe you have felt the same.

Paul writes in Ephesians 1:5 that God decided in advance to adopt us into his own family by bringing us to himself through Jesus Christ. This is what he wanted to do, and it gave him great pleasure. It was his choice and had nothing to do with our conduct. God didn't create a contract that we need to keep. Instead, he made a covenant with us, to love us as his children.

Before the creation of the world, God decided that he wanted us as his children. For us to become his children he sent Jesus from heaven to earth to live the perfect life, so that he could become the perfect sacrifice, so that through faith we could become perfect and holy. His only request is that we believe in the One he sent. Our right to be called his children are given through our faith in God's Son. I am a child of God because of my faith in Jesus Christ. As a child of God, I have been given a new identity that comes with the promise of God's eternal presence, protection, and provision.

Christian Churches Ireland runs a youth camp every summer called Pulse Camp. Several years ago I was asked to look after the keynote speaker Terry Parkman and his wife Christina, who oversee the Next Gen ministries of River Valley Church. They are the parents of two beautiful girls, Avalie and Nova. Both girls were born in China and were living in difficult circumstances when the Parkman's connected with them and decided to adopt them and make them their children. They have welcomed them into their family with loving and open arms, given them a new identity as the Parkman girls, and are helping them thrive in their new life. I love seeing the updates that both Christina and Terry post on their social media platforms. It's a reflection of God's heart for humanity. He wants to rescue us, position us in a loving family, and his church, and provide us with everything we need to thrive in life.

As children of God, we receive a new identity. We become citizens of heaven, and members of the family of God and begin the journey to become our true selves, living in the freedom Jesus won for us on the cross. Paul writes in his second letter to the church in Corinth that in Christ Jesus each one of us is a new creation, given the capacity to live, love, serve and grow just like him.

There are days when I still have to wrestle with this biblical truth. There are days when my mind will wander, when my past reminds me of who I was and attempts to pull me back into my old self, living defeated, lost, scared, ashamed, guilty, and afraid. I've been an addict and a thief. I've mugged people, burgled homes, robbed my family, and slept with people for financial, emotional, and physical gain. I've lied, cheated, conned, and insulted my nearest and dearest. For longer than I care to remember I was not a nice person and sometimes my head and heart can fall back into believing that's who I am. This is why the I AM statements included in this book have become so important to me. I have to constantly remind myself that I am no longer that person, that I've been given a new identity, and that I am indeed a child of God, clothed in robes of righteousness, forgiven, chosen, set apart, and filled with his Spirit and that everything I need for life and godliness has been given to me through the presence, provision, and protection of God.

Several years ago, my dad sat at my kitchen table and explained to me that for all of his life, he had felt like a woman trapped inside a man's body. He said that the next time I would see him he would be dressed as a woman and from that point on he would be engaged in a process that would see him receiving gender alignment surgery and embracing life as a female. As I'm sure you can appreciate, it was a very difficult time for both of us.

In the lead-up to meeting Frances for the first time, I was terrified. I was scared on so many different levels. I was anxious about how I would respond and what that would do to our relationship moving forward. I was grieving the loss of my father Frank. I was angry at the impact the situation was having on the rest of my family. It felt like an imposter had come in and torn us apart. I was nervous that I would say the wrong thing, or use the wrong pronoun. As I approached the door of the apartment where Frances was, I wanted to turn and run. It's amazing how at that moment,

God used my relationship with my dad Frank to help me walk towards the new relationship I was entering into with Frances. God's promise of his presence, provision, and protection came to light as I remembered moments of my childhood with Frank.

There is a beautiful beach in the northwest of Ireland called Portsalon Beach. We visited it quite a lot as a family when I was younger and would sometimes go wild camping there. One night my parents were in the camper van and my sister and I were in a tent beside them. In the small hours of the night, a group of drunk young adults thought it would be fun to come and shake the tent. My sister and I were terrified. We called out to my dad for help and he came bursting out of the van swinging a canoe paddle, if anyone had gotten in his way as he came to our rescue they would have lost their head. His presence brought comfort, his weapon made him stronger, and he provided a way for us to walk to safety and filled us with courage as we did. This is exactly what I needed to remember as I walked towards the door to meet Frances for the first time. It's the father's heart to be with us in times of trouble, to fill us with the confidence to walk through those times of trouble, and to offer protection as we do.

I've met a lot of people who are under the impression that as children of God, we are promised the absence of trouble, the absence of difficult circumstances, and the absence of challenges in life. With these false expectations comes a false sense of hope that typically leads to disappointment. False expectations unfortunately lead us to question our faith negatively.

The only expectations that Jesus ever met were those of the father. Jesus spent a lot of time challenging misconceptions and attitudes. He was very clear that we should expect trouble but he was also very clear that we would never be alone in that trouble. The good news is that God invites us to invite him into our trouble and promises to be with us as we call out to him. David describes it like this in Psalm 91 "When he calls out to Me, I will answer him; I will be with him in trouble. I will deliver him and honour him". God promises his children his presence and with his presence comes his protection.

I'm sure you can imagine that walking to the door to meet Frances for the first time was one of the most difficult environments and experiences that I've ever had to walk towards in my life. It felt like I was walking toward a symbolic lion's den.

In the first six chapters of the Old Testament book of Daniel, you will find two stories that detail the protection of God that accompanies the presence of God. In the first, you will find three young men Shadrach, Meshach, and Abednego who, after being thrown into a fiery furnace, find themselves divinely delivered. In the second, Daniel is thrown into a lion's den and again is divinely delivered. Their faith revealed God's favour towards them.

It takes faith to believe that we are children of God and through our faith, God reveals his favour towards us.

In his letter to the church in Rome, Paul writes "Because of our faith, Christ has brought us into this place of undeserved privilege where we now stand, and we confidently and joyfully look forward to sharing God's glory."
Romans 5:2 NLT

When Jennie and I decided to move to Omagh, we had to take several faith steps. One of those huge faith steps was telling the kids what we believed God had placed in our hearts and what he was leading us towards. We didn't exactly choose the best moment to inform them of our great news and if you ever need to share news with your children that is about to turn their lives upside down please choose a more appropriate moment than their birthday celebration dinner. The news went down like a lead balloon and was as welcome as a fart in a space suit. Our excitement wasn't mirrored in their responses. The kids were typically and understandably concerned about their friendships, family connections, and school setting. We were about to move to a new town in a different county where we didn't know anyone, with nothing but a message filled with hope that said your future is brighter than the darkness of your past. We believed that God was calling us to speak life, love, and hope into the heart of Omagh.

As children of God, we are children of promise.

We reminded the kids that we believed God would be with us, provide for us and protect us every step of the way. We shared Phillipians 4:19 with them and encouraged them to believe with us that God would meet all of our needs according to the riches of his glory in Christ Jesus.

Something very beautiful happened on the first day the twins went to school. We had agreed with them that we would be their chauffeurs until they settled into the new rhythm and established some new relationships. At the first school pick-up, the twins came home filled with joy and delight informing us that they would be making their own way home from school tomorrow, that they had made friends, and were feeling comfortable in their new environment. God had indeed met their needs. Their first day was a huge success and the friends they made that day are still their closest friends today.

Something miraculous takes place when we choose to recognise God as our father in heaven and put our trust in him. He fills us with the courage to take our faith steps and positions us in relationships in which our needs are met.

Exodus 14 paints a beautiful picture of what is available to the children of God as a result of the presence, protection, and provision of God. The Israelites have fled captivity from their Egyptian rulers and find themselves with a massive decision to make - trust God for their next step or face a return to their old way of life as slaves to Pharaoh. Their next step was a significant step of faith that required them to walk into the unknown and believe in a miracle. After a conversation with God, Moses raises his staff and the water separates and in doing so creates a pathway between two water walls. The Israelite people step onto the newly formed dry land and walk across to the other side. When they reach their place of safety God instructs Moses to raise his hand and the water closes in on top of the following Egyptians, destroying them. The Bible tells us that "not so much as one of them remained". (Exodus 14:28)

Their faith revealed the favour of God. Their faith led to the place of promise. Through their faith, they were repositioned from where they were to where God wanted them to be. As children of God, they were guided by God and they were protected by God. As children of the Lord Most High, they received his provision every day. God was with them every step of the way, he went before them, above them, and behind them, following them with goodness and mercy.

The biblical narrative has never changed. God loves his children and wants them to come home. He provides a pathway through faith in Jesus Christ. John 1:12 tells us, "Yet to all who did receive him, to those who believed in his name, he gave the right to become children of God".

The God of the Old Testament is the God of the New Testament and the God of the New Testament is the same yesterday, today, and forever. He is the God who promises to be with us regardless of whether we are in the valley, on the mountaintop, or somewhere in between. He is the God who promises to give us everything we need for the journey. He is the God who has put himself inside us and is leading his children home.

CHAPTER THREE

I AM FORGIVEN

God calls us to embrace the character of Christ and become people of grace and truth...

"He is so rich in kindness and grace that he purchased our freedom with the blood of his Son and forgave our sins." Ephesians 1:7 NLT

When the twins were born, Jennie and I decided to pack up our lives in Dublin and relocate to Liverpool. Jennie's dad was generous and offered to help us get on the property ladder and give me full-time employment in his motorcycle training and sales store. We bought a house and set up camp in a beautiful little town called Neston on the outskirts of the city. It was the fresh start that we had hoped for. Things took a turn for the worse when Jennie's mum, who had divorced her dad years earlier, became terminally ill and died. Jennie became quite depressed after the death of her mum. Unfortunately, I wasn't a great support to her. We grew apart and she fell into a relationship with my best friend. During this time Jennie fell pregnant and attempted suicide, and through this, I found out about the affair. We split up and I returned to Northern Ireland with the twins.

Upon our return, I rented a house for the three of us in my hometown of Derry. We rented from a company called O'Keefe Somerville Estate Agents. One of the senior partners was a gentleman named Brian Somerville. Brian agreed to let me pay 6 months' rent in advance and I moved in with the twins. At the end of those 6 months, I was unemployed and agreed with Brian that I would get assistance from the local housing executive to pay the rent. Unfortunately, due to a series of poor choices and severe procrastination, the necessary paperwork was not completed and after a lot of chasing from Brian, we were asked to vacate the property. When we handed back the keys, the property was in a much less beautiful state than when we had received it. We had broken windows, damaged carpets, and furniture and wrecked the place, dishonouring the opportunity we had been given to make this house our home.

When I started attending Cornerstone City Church, Brian became the Assistant Pastor. It was a massive challenge for me to be there with him. I was feeling guilty and embarrassed about how I had disrespected both him and his business. When I would see Brian coming, I would turn and walk in the opposite direction and so I managed to avoid eye contact with him for months. But I knew something had to change and so I called Brian's office to see if we could grab a coffee. We met in a coffee shop where I poured my heart out and apologised for my behaviour and asked Brian to forgive me. Brian responded most beautifully and reminded me that I was forgiven both by God and by him. He explained that his desires for me matched God's and that he wanted me to thrive. Brian then proceeded to invite me to his home that evening and planted me in the heart of the church.

Paul writes in Ephesians 1:7 (NLT) "He is so rich in kindness and grace that he purchased our freedom with the blood of his Son and forgave our sins."

Accepting forgiveness can be a very difficult thing for a lot of people. Many of us lack the compassion, humility, and patience to forgive ourselves and therefore we find it a challenge when others forgive us. This can have a massive impact on our relationship with God. Although we have been told that we are forgiven, many of us carry the guilt, shame, and remorse of our past sins, and our inability to forgive ourselves impacts our ability to connect with God.

In 2018 I was invited to be one of the keynote speakers at the MVMNT conference which was held at The Helix Centre in Dublin. The Helix is one of Ireland's premier entertainment venues and it happens to be the venue in which the television program The Voice Ireland is filmed and recorded. The Voice is a reality tv singing program in which contestants come onto the stage to sing for judges who have their backs turned. The judges sit in high-backed red chairs, and if they like the voice of the contestant they can press a button that will turn their chair around, which signals to the contestant that they have been accepted. I can imagine that for a lot of contestants, the journey from the dressing room to the stage and all through the performance has the potential to be a very anxious time. Wondering if our performance is going to be good enough for us to be accepted in any area of life can create anxiety and stress. Imagine what it would be like to step onto the stage wondering whether or not someone will turn, whether or not our performance would be good enough to get us accepted.

So many people in the Christian Church continue to bring that same performance-based anxiety into their relationship with God. This belief system stems from our inability to accept and receive the forgiveness Christ won for us on the cross. It causes us to live in such a way that we assume God made a contract with us rather than a covenant. God's forgiveness was not and is not determined by our ability to stick to the obligations of a contract. God's forgiveness was won for us on the cross as a result of a covenant God made with his people.

"The days are coming," declares the Lord, "when I will make a new covenant with the people of Israel and with the people of Judah. It will not be like the covenant I made with their ancestors when I took them by the hand to lead them out of Egypt, because they broke my covenant, though I was a husband to them, " declares the Lord. "This is the covenant I will make with the people of Israel after that time," declares the Lord. "I will put my law in their minds and write it on their hearts. I will be their God, and they will be my people. No longer will they teach their neighbour, or say to one another, 'Know the Lord,' because they will all know me, from the least of them to the greatest," declares the Lord. "For I will forgive their wickedness and will remember their sins no more."
Jeremiah 31:31-34 NIV

Our ability to receive forgiveness is deeply rooted in our understanding of who God is and what we believe about him.

The most important question you will ever have to answer and keep answering regularly, is this: "What do I believe about God?". I have to question my God theology every day. I ask myself most mornings what I believe and why I believe it. I have several fundamental non-negotiables. They are the foundation of my faith. I can't comprehend the world coming into existence by accident. If the world came into existence by accident that essentially makes you and me an accident. You are way too beautiful, and we are too alike, for it to be accidental. I believe Jesus was and is the saviour of the world. After watching the movie, The Case for Christ, I do not doubt that Jesus walked the earth. Taking everything he said into account he will fit into one of three categories: liar, lunatic, or lord. I can't comprehend humanity allowing itself to be shaped for thousands of years by either a lunatic or a liar and therefore I believe him to be lord. I am convinced that God loves me and that God is for me.

Because I am convinced of these things, I am better positioned to believe everything God has said about me and written for me.

As a parent and as a child I have seen the power that forgiveness can bring. I have first-hand experience with what it means to both give and receive forgiveness. As a child I broke my mothers heart. I lied, stole, manipulated, attacked, and disappeared regularly. Shame often drove me away and guilt often kept me away. Guilt and shame have the potential to lead us into isolation.

Forgiveness has the opposite effect. Forgiveness has the potential to lead to reconciliation which in turn can lead to restoration. I've lost count of the number of times my parents' forgiveness led to the restoration of our broken relationship. What my parents modelled has impacted my parenting most positively. Love never fails. My desire for my children is straightforward, that they would know they can always come home because they are loved. God's desire for you is a mirror of this: he wants his children to come home and he wants them to know that they are loved.

Many people in western society will be almost too familiar with the bible story of the Prodigal Son found in the New Testament. The Parable of the Prodigal Son, also known as the parable of the Forgiving Father, tells the story of two sons and their father. One of the sons demands his inheritance from the father and then runs off and squanders the money living the high life. He ends up in the gutter and allows his guilt and shame to keep him separated from his family. He lives as a slave and eventually finds the courage to return home. Upon his return, he is met by his father who welcomes him home with open arms and proceeds to invite him to return to his place in the family as his son.

Both sons are massively challenged by the father's response. Both sons agree that the Prodigal Son doesn't deserve to receive the father's forgiveness but the father's desire to forgive his son and restore their relationship is overwhelming. It's a beautiful picture of grace in action.

Grace rarely makes sense - it's messy, it's unfair and it's rarely if ever, deserved. Grace is unmerited favour. I believe that our inability to accept and receive forgiveness is deeply rooted in our misunderstanding of grace. Equally, our ability to forgive is rooted in our ability to understand grace.

The theme of grace is continuously woven throughout the biblical narrative. God's children mess up, there is a breakdown in the relationship, God unconditionally forgives and the relationship is restored.

The Bible teaches us that we cannot out-sin God's forgiveness and we cannot outrun his goodness and mercy. It's always following us and it will be with us forever. **It takes great faith to receive forgiveness and even greater faith to live forgiven.** Believing in the grace of God is an act of faith that will change our lives if we will allow it.

"For it is by grace you have been saved, through faith—and this is not from yourselves, it is the gift of God. "
Ephesians 2:8

If we can have the faith to believe that God is who he says he is, then surely we can find the faith to believe in what he says he has done.

My very limited understanding of forgiveness and my limited ability to accept and receive forgiveness have had a huge impact on my interpersonal relationships. It's no secret that my life was completely turned upside down, that I was massively grieved and deeply hurt when my relationship with Jennie broke down. I was angry, I was bitter, I was resentful and for the longest time, the last thing on my mind was forgiveness. I grieved the loss of our relationship and resented the impact it would have on our children and their future.

I want to repeat myself in saying that I am not perfect and certainly not without fault. I cannot point the finger of fault solely at Jennie and must accept the fact that it was our relationship and whilst I felt massively wronged at that moment, there is no question that some of my attitudes, actions, and behaviours would have hurt Jennie.

It's easy to be a person of truth when you are the person that's been wronged. It's not so easy to be a person of grace when you are the person that's been wronged. Yet, God calls us to embrace the character of Christ and become people of grace and truth. **Grace doesn't mean that we ignore the truth, in fact, grace is revealed because of truth.**

After our initial split, Jennie and I lived separate lives and pursued new relationships for several years. Then there came the defining moment that brought us back together and was the catalyst for the life we now live together.

Jennie and I both made a commitment to follow Jesus to the ends of the earth, were members of the same church, attended the same groups, and had 3 beautiful children together. In all of those opportunities for communication and reconciliation, we totally missed the mark to the point that other people were uncomfortable in our company. I think it's fair to say that we both became increasingly uncomfortable about how we were making other people uncomfortable, and we decided to confront the elephant in the room. We arranged to meet for dinner in a local restaurant. We were both anxious about the encounter and certainly didn't expect to leave the restaurant in the way that we did. We entered the restaurant as enemies and left as the future Mr & Mrs. Shiels. Over that three hours, we knew we were going to spend the rest of our lives together.

What happened on that night was a miracle and to this day it's possibly the greatest miracle I've ever seen in my life. We were so far apart and yet in the blink of an eye God pulled and pushed us together and made a pathway of forgiveness for us to walk across.

If we are to forgive, we must give up the rights we feel we have to punish the person who has offended us. If we are to forgive, we must be prepared to wrestle with the emotions we experience, in such a way that they do not control us and create a barrier to the pathway forgiveness creates. If we are to forgive, we must accept that we too are flawed and require forgiveness in our own lives.

Once you were alienated from God and were enemies in your minds because of your evil behaviour. But now he has reconciled you by Christ's physical body through death to present you holy in his sight, without blemish and free from accusation...
Colossians 1:21 - 22

I have several habits that I perform daily that I believe have led me to become a better disciple, husband, father, communicator, and athlete. One of them is my daily office - the ancient Christian practice of beginning and ending each day with Bible reading and prayer. Most mornings I pray the following words from Psalm 139 before breaking bread in a time of private communion.

"Search me, O God, and know my heart; test me and know my anxious thoughts. Point out anything in me that offends

you, and leads me along the path of everlasting life."
Psalms 139:23-24 NLT

It amazes me how often God will highlight an area of my life in which I am carrying unforgiveness. It equally amazes me how in those moments the gentle touch of the Holy Spirit restores and refreshes my mind, heart, and soul.

Forgiveness leads to forgiveness.

God is good.

CHAPTER FOUR

I AM FREE

Jesus invites us to wait with him, to wait on him, to work with him and walk with him as he leads us into fresh revelation and new-found freedom...

"It is for freedom that Christ has set us free. Stand firm, then, and do not let yourselves be burdened again by a yoke of slavery." Galatians 5:1 NIV

I hit a wall as I began to dream about this chapter. I've spent eight weeks wrestling with the chapter title alone. I am massively challenged by the idea of living free and being free. I know what the bible teaches about freedom but I wonder if I truly believe that I am free. As I begin to imagine what it is to be free, I'm reminded that there are several visible areas in my life that need to reflect the glory of the freedom won for me on the cross of Jesus Christ.

I have reconciled myself to the fact that, although I am free, there are still some areas in my life where I am finding freedom. Therefore, a more authentic chapter title that reflects my current state would be: I am finding freedom.

The idea of being free and finding true freedom is ultimately connected to our relationships. There are some relationships in which we feel a greater sense of freedom than others. Freedom for me is the ability to live as my authentic self, the person Jesus died for me to become while living the life he died for me to have.

I believe the process of finding freedom is similar to the process of sanctification. Hebrews 10:10 tells us that because of Christ's sacrifice, we have been made holy. But we know that there are areas in our lives that don't reflect the holiness we read about in the scriptures. In the eyes of

God, we have been made holy but in our humanity, we are being made holy. I find it comforting to know that I am already free while also still finding freedom.

I would describe myself as a professional introvert. I am quite comfortable being in the spotlight when necessary but I prefer not to be the centre of attention if I can avoid it. I am an elite-level master's athlete. I love athletics. But it might shock you to learn that, in the last six years, I have travelled to twenty-eight races and finished only five. I experience horrific anxiety that paralyses me and prevents me from making it to the start line, never mind the finish line.

For most of my life, I have believed that I am a natural introvert. But I've grown to understand that, while there is some truth in that, it's not the whole truth. There are areas in my life that have conditioned me to become more introverted than God designed me to be.

Past hurts have the potential to cause us to withdraw and leave us living our lives in isolation. They also have the potential to lead us into developing performance-based anxiety that will also lock us in self-imposed prisons. This prevents us from living in the freedom that Jesus won for us on the cross.

I love running, yet on race day I would prefer to hide in my car than race on the track. On paper, I am one of the best 800m runners in the world, so having fear in this area doesn't make sense. This fear has such deep roots that I cannot reach them by myself.

Paul writes these words to the Galatian Church:

"It is for freedom that Christ has set us free. Stand firm, then, and do not let yourselves be burdened again by a yoke of slavery." Galatians 5:1

If I ask you to identify your yoke of slavery, the thing that is holding you back, you may find it difficult to do so. You may be aware of the area where the issue arises, but you may not be aware of the thoughts or circumstances to which the root is connected. It is possible that you do not have the language to communicate the very thing that is holding you captive.

The good news for the children of God is that God wants to partner with us in helping us find freedom. Without belittling our experiences, I want you and I to be encouraged in knowing that the pathway to our freedom is simpler than we think.

Our freedom is found in our following.

I often contemplate the level of freedom Peter must have experienced when he walked on water. At that moment I assume he was free from any sense of limitation or sense of expectation.

Matthew 14 describes the experience like this:

"Immediately Jesus made the disciples get into the boat and go on ahead of him to the other side, while he dismissed the crowd. After he had dismissed them, he went up to a mountainside by himself to pray. Later that night, he was there alone, and the boat was already a considerable distance from land, buffeted by the waves because the wind was against it.

Shortly before dawn, Jesus went out to them, walking on the lake. When the disciples saw him walking on the lake, they were terrified. "It's a ghost," they said and cried out in fear.

But Jesus immediately said to them: "Take courage! It is I. Don't be afraid."

"Lord, if it's you," Peter replied, "tell me to come to you on the water."

"Come," he said.

Then Peter got down out of the boat, walked on the water, and came toward Jesus. But when he saw the wind, he was afraid and, beginning to sink, cried out, "Lord, save me!"

Immediately Jesus reached out his hand and caught him. "You of little faith," he said, "why did you doubt?"

And when they climbed into the boat, the wind died down. Then those who were in the boat worshiped him, saying, "Truly you are the Son of God."

During that life-changing moment, we see two key elements at work in Peter's life. Firstly, he was in the presence of God. Secondly, he stood on the word of God. This teaches us that true freedom is found through the combination of the presence of God and the word of God in our lives.

Our youngest daughter has just started High School. Before Jennie's pregnancy with Cadhla, we had several miscarriages. Those were dark days, so dark that during the first trimester, I refused to accept that Jennie was carrying a healthy baby and would give birth to a beautiful child. I had been hurt before and didn't want to be hurt again. I had to pick up the pieces before and I didn't want to have to do it again while wrestling with my grief. It felt safer to remain trapped in my self-imposed prison than to risk stepping out and embracing the freedom and joy a new parent can have.

Several weeks into the second trimester I was out on a training run. This was no ordinary training run, it was a life-changing supernatural encounter. As I ran down the road about three miles from our home, I heard a voice, as clear as the sun in the sky on a summer's day, say, "Tim, what do you want your daughter to look like?". I looked around, a little freaked out, and couldn't see another human being. The voice spoke again. This time I knew it was God. I proceeded to have a conversation with God that has impacted my life forever. I ran home in record time and told Jennie what had happened. We knew we were having a girl and we knew we would call her Cadhla.

Something very special happened at that moment. God's words released me from the prison cell and set me free to be the husband Jennie needed and the father my children needed, both born and unborn.

Imagine the God of the universe being so interested in the details of our lives that he would hijack our daily routine to get our attention and breathe life into our souls.

In John's gospel, Jesus is quoted as saying, "If you hold my teaching you are my disciples. Then you will know the truth and the truth will set you free."
John 8:31-32

Both the word of God and the Spirit of God will always lead us to freedom.

When a prisoner is released they are led from their prison cell by a prison officer who leads them to freedom. For many prisoners, their time in captivity causes them to become institutionalised. Their habits and thought patterns are influenced by their environment and, if these are not changed, the prisoner will remain a prisoner even though they have been set free. They may be free but they need to learn how to live free. This is why the word of God is essential in helping us find freedom because it teaches us how to live free.

Paul writes these words to his young apprentice Timothy to remind him of this.

"All Scripture is God-breathed [given by divine inspiration] and is profitable for instruction, for conviction [of sin], for correction [of error and restoration to obedience], for training in righteousness [learning to live in conformity to God's will, both publicly and privately—behaving honourably with personal integrity and moral courage."
2 Timothy 3:16

Several years ago I had a fresh revelation of what it means to be a person of Spirit and truth. I realised that to be Spirit-led I needed to be word-filled. To have confidence in the leading of the Holy Spirit, I needed a deep understanding of what the scriptures say about the character of God. This would allow me to follow the Spirit without fear. The Spirit of God will never contradict the word of God and vice versa.

In my quest for freedom, I try to remember the following four things. Firstly, trust the process. Secondly, have patience and wait on God. Thirdly, put on the armour of God. Finally, stay in the presence of God.

When Jesus died on the cross, the sins of the world died with him. Our freedom is found in him. Those who are in Christ are new creations, no longer slaves to their sins. Jesus lived the perfect life so that he could be the perfect sacrifice to set us free. That once-and-for-all sacrifice that makes us holy enables us, in our broken humanity, to encounter God in his great divinity. Christ's sacrifice allows us the privilege of having the freedom to approach God's throne of grace with confidence.

Let me ask you a question :

How do you approach God?

Do you approach his throne of grace with fear, and does that fear impact your ability to bring your authentic self before him, because you too are afraid that you will be rejected?

Here's some more good news for you, **Freedom was won for us on the cross. Freedom is given to us through the cross. We find our freedom at the foot of the cross.** Everything we need for life and godliness is made available to us because of the cross. This means that we are free to present our authentic broken selves before God without fear of rejection.

Having the freedom to be with God permits us to wait with God.

I have discovered that waiting is not a passive activity. Waiting is intentional and one expects something to change. If you think about it, when you wait at a red traffic light, you're not passive, you're intentional and expectant. You wait expecting change to come so that you can continue with your journey.

In Psalm 27:13-14 the author details the expectancy and intentionality of waiting like this, "I remain confident of this: I will see the goodness of the Lord in the land of the living. Wait for the Lord; be strong, take heart, and wait for the Lord."

Jesus invites us to wait with him, to wait on him, to work with him, and walk with him as he leads us into fresh revelation and new-found freedom. Revelation brings freedom and faith accesses it, pushing us towards the preferred future God has for us, that Christ's death on the cross has secured for us.

As we access our freedom and step into our future it's important to remember that the enemy of our souls is prowling like a lion and looking for someone to devour. He wants to inhibit our ability to find freedom and live free. Peter reminds us to be vigilant and Paul reminds us to wear the spiritual armour God has given us.

After encouraging the church in Ephesus and reminding them of the spiritual blessings made available to them through faith in Jesus Christ, Paul writes this:

"Finally, be strong in the Lord and his mighty power. Put on the full armour of God, so that you can take your stand against the devil's schemes. For our struggle is not against flesh and blood, but against the rulers, against the authorities, against the powers of this dark world, and the spiritual forces of evil in the heavenly realms. Therefore put on the full armour of God, so that when the day of evil comes, you may be able to stand your ground, and after you have done everything, stand. Stand firm then, with the belt of truth buckled around your waist, with the breastplate of righteousness in place, and with your feet fitted with the readiness that comes from the gospel of peace. In addition to all this, take up the shield of faith, with which you can extinguish all the flaming arrows of the evil one. Take the helmet of salvation and the sword of the Spirit, which is the word of God. And pray in the Spirit on all occasions with all kinds of prayers and requests. With this in mind, be alert and always keep on praying for all the Lord's people."
Ephesians 6:10-18 NIV

The kingdom of God is where freedom reigns. Wherever God is, there is freedom. The Bible teaches us in 2 Corinthians, "Now the Lord is the Spirit, and where the Spirit of the Lord is, there is freedom" (2 Cor 3:17). It, therefore, makes sense to me that freedom is found in the passionate pursuit of God.

Here's a thought: what if, instead of chasing after freedom, we just chased after God?

Imagine what your life would look like if you chose to do that...

CHAPTER FIVE

I AM NEVER ALONE

Imagine what your life would look like if you truly believed that God was with you in every moment of every day, in every place and space you inhabit...

"I can never escape from your Spirit! I can never get away from your presence." Psalm 139:7 NLT

In the late 1970s and early 1980s most coastal towns in Ireland were always a hive of activity. These were the days when budget airlines were nothing but a dream and foreign holidays were reserved for the elite of society. Growing up in the border town of Derry meant that we were spoiled for choice. We were less than thirty minutes from the sea in any direction. Our favourite place was a Donegal town called Buncrana. Nestled right in the middle of the Inishowen peninsula, it has the most stunning sea views. If you lived in the northwest of Ireland, it was the place to be. There was a season in the wider Shiels family when my dad was the only person who had a car. Being the only driver and car owner, he was often tasked with bringing the whole family to Buncrana. Bearing in mind that this was a time when road safety laws were quite relaxed, we might have had as many as ten possibly twelve people in the car on any one trip.

On one particular trip, while in Cullens Amusements, I got separated from the wider group. Essentially, the group had lost me. I was five years old at the time. My family remembers the events that happened afterward much more vividly than I do. I'm sure you can appreciate the level of fear and anxiety any family would experience, having lost a child in their care. As events unfolded, the whole town was on high alert looking for the missing child.

My dad found me sitting on the car bonnet (hood if you're American). I was the picture of peace as I sat staring into space, seemingly without a care in the world. My dad has told me on numerous occasions that he could see that I was at peace. He proceeded to ask me if I had been afraid and was shocked when I responded " why would I be afraid when God was right here with me ?"

Something beautiful happens when we recognise that God is with us. His presence comforts us, strengthens us, and fills us with courage. It gives us joy and a peace that is beyond anything we could dream or imagine for ourselves.

The Old Testament book of Exodus gives great insight into the leading, constructive, and encouraging relational essence of God's presence in our lives. Moses had numerous encounters with God. He talked to God. He rested in God. He received instruction from God. He saw the glory of God and worshipped him. He repented before God. He received promises from God. He was transformed by God and equipped for service. He grew in confidence both with God and in God.

I've already told you this in a previous chapter but it was such a huge moment that I want to address it again. The first time I went to visit my dad after he had transitioned from Frank to Frances, from male to female was a very scary moment in my life. I had no idea what to expect and no idea how I would respond. I was terrified. As I walked towards the door of the apartment he was staying in, I was comforted by this thought. **The God I'm walking with is the God I'm walking to.** I'm comforted in knowing that

God was with me as I walked towards the door and was already waiting for me on the other side of the door. I was stepping in peace, I was walking in rest and to rest. My God would not forsake me.

God's promise that "I will never leave you nor forsake you" is found in multiple books of the Bible, in both the Old and New Testaments. It's a promise that is enforced through the biblical narrative.

The Psalmist David knew it when he penned these words. "Where can I go from your Spirit? Where can I flee from your presence? If I go up to the heavens, you are there; if I make my bed in the depths, you are there. If I rise on the wings of the dawn, if I settle on the far side of the sea, even there your hand will guide me, your right hand will hold me."
Psalm 139:7-10

Most commentators, theologians, and bible scholars point to these verses when attempting to explain or describe God as omnipresent. Simply put, omnipresent is the quality of being everywhere. Believing in the omnipresence of God is super important because, if you want to believe that God is with you, you must first believe he is omnipresent. Believing that you're never alone rests upon this biblical truth.

Imagine what your life would look like if you truly believed that God was with you in every moment of every day, every place and space you inhabit. It has the potential to change everything about the way you live your life.

For several years, I had the privilege of leading a thriving children's ministry team called The Extreme Team. We traveled around primary schools sharing biblical truths in a fun and vibrant way. In Derry, it would have been unusual for a lot of children at the time not to have met us at some point. During my first few weeks on the team, I noticed something very unusual happen when I would visit our local shopping centre. As I would navigate my way through the shopping aisles, I began to notice that children would point at me and bring my presence to the attention of their parents. My position on the team now meant that I had to become increasingly aware of my behaviour, attitudes, and responses when in public due to the eyes that would be watching my every move. It's amazing how quickly your behaviour will change when you know you are being watched.

I don't mean to suggest that God is sitting on his heavenly throne, watching your every move, waiting to poke you with a holy pitchfork if your human behaviour doesn't align with his great divinity. However, if you think about this for a minute, how would your behaviour change if your awareness of his presence increased? Would you be more courageous? less anxious? kinder? slower to react angrily? Would you gossip? Would you look at that website?

Imagine how both your public and private life would change if you believed that God was with you everywhere you go.

Tim Hughes is a tremendous worship leader and songwriter. In 2007 he wrote one of my favourite songs to sing. The lyrics read like this

God in my living
There in my breathing
God in my waking
God in my sleeping
God in my resting
There in my working
God in my thinking
God in my speaking

Be my everything
Be my everything
Be my everything
Be my everything

God in my hoping
There in my dreaming
God in my watching
God in my waiting
God in my laughing
There in my weeping
God in my hurting
God in my healing

Christ in me
Christ in me
Christ in me the hope of glory
You are everything
Christ in me

Christ in me
Christ in me the hope of glory
Be my everything

I love the idea of God being in everything and being my everything. I love that I not only stand in his presence but that I also carry his presence with me everywhere I go.

In his first letter to the church in Corinth, Paul writes "All of you surely know you are God's temple and his Spirit lives in you." That's a pretty extraordinary piece of scripture right there. Not only is he everywhere I go because of his omnipresent nature but he's also everywhere I go because he is in me. As children of God, we carry the great comforter with us everywhere we go. We carry the God of strength, joy, and hope with us everywhere we go. Like seriously, how incredibly awesome is that?

My youngest daughter Cadhla is a Liverpool Football Club supporter. During the summer, as a treat, she and I went to Liverpool for a few days. While there, we visited Anfield Stadium, the home of Liverpool F.C. We also visited a store called Build-A-Bear. If you have young children or grandchildren, I recommend a visit. They have a store in most major cities. It's a wonderful shopping experience that allows you to build and customise your teddy bear. You get to choose what the bear looks like and what goes into the bear, including its heart.

I'm not going to belittle your Christian experience to a Build-A-Bear shop. However, while in the store it became a beautiful reminder of what happens to us when we are born again as children of God and become part of the family of God. God gives us a new heart, fills us with his spirit, and sends us out into the world to live the life Jesus died for us to have.

The God that surrounds us with his peace has put his peace inside of us and commanded us to bring it to the ends of the earth. The God that comforts us has filled us with compassion and called us to love one another, in the way that he loves us.

God's presence in our lives, radiating through our lives, has a very specific purpose. In the same way that we know that we are not alone, God uses his presence in us to tell the world that they too are not alone. We love because he loved and loves us. We forgive because he has forgiven us. We serve because he served us. We carry his presence because he has given us his presence.

The beautiful thing about the presence of God is that it will always lead us toward the promises of God. You can read this and see it unfold in the Old Testament book of Ezekiel.

"""" 'For I will take you out of the nations; I will gather you from all the countries and bring you back into your own land. I will sprinkle clean water on you, and you will be clean; I will cleanse you from all your impurities and from all your idols. I will give you a new heart and put a new spirit in you; I will remove from you your heart of stone and give you a heart of flesh. And I will put my Spirit in you and move you to follow my decrees and be careful to

keep my laws. Then you will live in the land I gave your ancestors; you will be my people, and I will be your God."
Ezekiel 36:24-28 NIV

Once again the nation of Israel find itself on the receiving end of God's unmerited favour. They've been disobedient, yet once again God is calling them home. Calling them back to himself. That's what God does, he calls us home. I have even more good news for you, **God's desire for you to be in his presence will always surpass any desire you have to be in his presence.** He demonstrated the level of desire he had by allowing Jesus to die the death that we deserved. Jesus' act of obedience cancels out every act of disobedience from the children of God. Those who die with Christ are then raised to new life in Christ, guaranteed God's presence in their lives for eternity.

In his letter to the church in Rome, the apostle Paul writes "Who shall separate us from the love of Christ? Shall trouble or hardship or persecution or famine or nakedness or danger or sword? As it is written: "For your sake, we face death all day long; we are considered as sheep to be slaughtered." No, in all these things we are more than conquerors through him who loved us. For I am convinced that neither death nor life, neither angels nor demons, neither the present nor the future, nor any powers, neither height nor depth, nor anything else in all creation, will be able to separate us from the love of God that is in Christ Jesus our Lord."
Romans 8:35-39 NIV

The more time I've spent trying to imagine life and understanding that I am never alone, the more encouraged I become. My mind has been blown wide open with this one thing. I am never alone.

It is easy sometimes to feel alone but sometimes our feelings will fool us. When I found myself at my crossroad in Dec 2019, I'm not sure I have ever felt more alone. Funny thing is, I was never alone and the presence of God was there to call me home. It wasn't that I had lost hope, I just couldn't see it. It wasn't that I had lost joy, I just couldn't see it. It wasn't that I had lost peace, I just couldn't see it. It wasn't that I had lost God's presence, I just couldn't see it.   I was blind to the very thing that was staring me in the face and had lost sight of who and what was available. My view was hindered and my thinking was stinking.

I now understand why the writer of Hebrews wrote "Therefore since we are surrounded by such a great cloud of witnesses, let us throw off everything that hinders and the sin that so easily entangles. And let us run with perseverance the race marked out for us, fixing our eyes on Jesus, the pioneer, and perfecter of faith. For the joy set before him, he endured the cross, scorning its shame, and sat down at the right hand of the throne of God. Consider him who endured such opposition from sinners, so that you will not grow weary and lose heart."
Hebrews 12:1-3 NIV

It's easy to lose your focus when you remove yourself from fellowship. In the rush of everyday life, it's easy to neglect time in fellowship, But here's the thing, if you're too busy for fellowship you are simply far too busy. What I mean by fellowship is this, investing in life-giving relationships in a life-giving church. I hit the self-destruct button the day I decided I was too busy for fellowship. It's very easy to feel alone when we start to neglect fellowship. It's very easy to become isolated when we stop investing in life-giving relationships. It's very easy to be attacked when we are separated from the pack.

I'm confident the writer of Hebrews knew this when writing this "Therefore, brothers and sisters, since we have the confidence to enter the Most Holy Place by the blood of Jesus, by a new and living way opened for us through the curtain, that is, his body, and since we have a great priest over the house of God, let us draw near to God with a sincere heart and with the full assurance that faith brings, having our hearts sprinkled to cleanse us from a guilty conscience and having our bodies washed with pure water. Let us hold unswervingly to the hope we profess, for he who promised is faithful. And let us consider how we may spur one another on toward love and good deeds, not giving up meeting together, as some are in the habit of doing, but encouraging one another—and all the more as you see the Day approaching."
Hebrews 10:19-25 NIV

CHAPTER SIX

I AM SAVED

In God's eyes we are too valuable not to save, too valuable not to redeem, too valuable not to restore and too valuable not to use...

"In him, we have redemption through his blood, the forgiveness of sins, in accordance with the riches of God's grace". Ephesians 1:7 NIV

Most people have a favourite tv program they get excited about. I love restoration programs, in which people go searching through other people's junk to restore whatever they find. I like programs such as American Pickers and Car SOS but my favourite is called Money for Nothing. The title itself is intriguing. The program is based around entrepreneur Sarah Moore saving things from being dumped, and then transforming them into valuable pieces, making money for people who had no idea there was cash to be made from their trash. Sarah travels the UK visiting local dumps, identifies items with hidden value, and saves them from the scrap heap. My favourite thing about her is her ability to see value in things that others have deemed worthless.

In Ephesians 1:7, Paul writes, "In him, we have redemption through his blood, the forgiveness of sins, in accordance with the riches of God's grace".
Ephesians 1:7 NIV

Through the blood of Jesus Christ, shed on the cross of Calvary, God saved us from the spiritual scrap heap, forgiving all our sins - past, present, and future.

In God's eyes, we are too valuable not to save, too valuable not to redeem, too valuable not to restore, and too valuable not to use. He wanted to show us this by demonstrating his love towards us, so while we were still sinners, while we were at our worst, he sent his son from heaven to earth, to die on a cross that we deserved, so that through faith we could be saved.

I have a few people in my life that I aspire to be like, one of them being Alan Graham, otherwise known as "The Good News Man". Alan recently came to Omagh Community Church and shared with us the story of how he would greet his work colleagues every morning at Shorts Factory in Belfast after encountering the saving grace and power of God. Every morning he would walk onto the shop floor and go towards his workstation singing the following words, " I am saved and I know that I am, I am saved and I know that I am, I am saved and I know that I am, I am glad that I know I am saved". I'm not going to lie to you. I doubt you'll ever see me strutting my stuff, walking around with the confidence of Alan but I have great confidence in knowing that I AM saved, who saved me, and what he saved me for. God is in the business of saving people.

In his book, Gospel Fluency, Jeff Vanderstelt reminds us that "we are saved from the penalty of sin, being saved from the power of sin, and will be saved from the presence of sin".

In the past, I've misunderstood what it means to be saved. Maybe, like me, you too have made the mistake of thinking that being saved was your 'get out of jail' or 'get into heaven' pass. Maybe as a result you have missed out on the now power of the gospel made available to us when we choose to follow Jesus. Jesus' invitation to follow him is so much more than a simple invitation. It is a call to purpose, a pathway for his plan, and a platform for his promises to you to come to life. It is an opportunity for a relationship, a passage to freedom, and an avenue to grace.

I believe with all of my heart that God has a preferred future for you that Jesus died on the cross to secure for you.

The Bible is packed full of the promises that God has made to his children. In the Old Testament book of Exodus, God makes a promise to save his children.

"Therefore, say to the Israelites: 'I am the Lord, and I will bring you out from under the yoke of the Egyptians. I will free you from being slaves to them, and I will redeem you with an outstretched arm and with mighty acts of judgment. I will take you as my own people, and I will be your God. Then you will know that I am the Lord your God, who brought you out from under the yoke of the Egyptians. And I will bring you to the land I swore with uplifted hand to give to Abraham, to Isaac and to Jacob. I will give it to you as a possession. I am the Lord.'"
Exodus 6: 6-8 NIV

God made a promise to the nation of Israel while they were enslaved in Egypt. He promised that he would save them, he promised that he would teach them to live saved, he promised that they would have a purpose in life, and he promised them intimacy with him. He brought them out from the authority of one kingdom to position them in another, and he promises to do the same with us. God promises to bring us out from under the authority of the kingdom of darkness and position us in his kingdom of light.

I've come to realise that being saved and living saved are two very different things.

The Foyle Bridge in Derry is a beautiful sight. It was built in such a way that large ships could pass underneath. Given its height, it has become a magnet for men and women in the northwest seeking to commit suicide. Several years ago I found myself at a crossroads in life, at the bridge, contemplating life and death. I was in a very dark place, completely burned out and massively suicidal. I had lost sight of who I was as a disciple, husband, father, communicator, and athlete. I was saved but I wasn't living saved. I had lost sight of the hope I carried.

The journey to this dark place began years before. In October 2016 I was honoured to represent Ireland at the World Masters Athletics Championships which were held in Perth, Western Australia. I was competing in the 800 metres and I was placed fourth in the m40 final. Most people reading this will be greatly impressed by a fourth-place finish at world level. At the time I believed that I had failed miserably. I truly believed that I was favourite to win, I had trained for 4 years to win and didn't. Because I had failed, I felt like a failure and quickly fell into the trap of believing I was indeed a failure. What we do should never determine who we are but on this occasion I allowed those feelings of failure to impact every area of my life. In an effort to counterbalance those feelings of negativity, I got busy. I attempted to excel in every area of my life. I began to perform for God rather than partner with him. In my head, I was running for him hoping that I would work through the negative feelings, but the opposite happened. I found myself in a place where I was so busy that I had become a stranger to my wife, my family, and my church. I became so disconnected that I believed both they and the world would be much better off without me.

God is most definitely more interested in our partnership with him than our performance for him.

I had to come to the end of myself to fully appreciate the enormity of that spiritual truth.

As I stood at the crossroads contemplating life and death I was reminded of another spiritual truth.

God will never let us down.

I bet there have been times in your life when it has felt like he has let you down, and it hurt. I've had times in my own life when it's felt like that. I've also had countless times when I have experienced the faithfulness of God when I have known his presence, power, provision, and protection. These are the memories that saved my life. As I contemplated my future, I realised that I hadn't lost hope, I'd just lost sight of it. I had allowed my disappointment, shame, anxiety, anger, frustration, and fear to impact my perception of my relationship with God. God had already saved me from a life of addiction, homelessness, broken relationships, and a list of hurts and pains, and I believed he could do it again. I found hope and began to walk in the freedom he had won for me on the cross.

My journey to becoming healthier began with a decision. I wanted to become a fitter, faster, stronger, healthier version of myself. You would be forgiven at this point, given my athletic background, for thinking these things would focus on physical application. They went much deeper than that. I wanted to be fitter. I wanted to build resilience again, understanding that perseverance would be a great quality to develop. I wanted to be faster. I wanted to respond quickly to the voice of God, the needs of others, and the cry of my soul. I wanted to be stronger. I wanted to delight myself in the Lord, recognising him as my source of strength. I wanted to be healthier. Nothing derailed my forward momentum more than my unhealthy thoughts. I wanted to begin again to take every thought captive and allow Jesus to transform my mind. I wanted to improve my mental health. At the heart of it all, there was a burning desire to learn to live saved again. I wanted to reposition myself from where I was to where I believed God wanted me to be.

I have a couple of passages of scripture that continue to have great application to my life. The first chapter of the Old Testament book of Joshua is one such passage that God continues to use to bring healing to my world. The passage gives tremendous insight into the strategy we can apply to our lives, should we have the desire to reposition ourselves from where we are to where we want to be.

The passage opens up with God giving Joshua the task of leading the Israelites from their wilderness experience into the promised land. I love this passage. God not only details the promise, but he also details the pathway.

1 After the death of Moses the servant of the Lord, the Lord said to Joshua son of Nun, Moses' aide: 2 "Moses my servant is dead. Now then, you and all these people, get ready to cross the Jordan River into the land I am about to give to them—to the Israelites. 3 I will give you every place where you set your foot, as I promised Moses. 4 Your territory will extend from the desert to Lebanon, and from the great river, the Euphrates—all the Hittite country—to the Mediterranean Sea in the west. 5 No one will be able to stand against you all the days of your life. As I was with Moses, so I will be with you; I will never leave you nor forsake you. 6 Be strong and courageous, because you will lead these people to inherit the land I swore to their ancestors to give them.7 "Be strong and very courageous. Be careful to obey all the law my servant Moses gave you; do not turn from it to the right or to the left, that you may be successful wherever you go. 8 Keep this Book of the Law always on your lips; meditate on it day and night, so that you may be careful to do everything written in it. Then you will be prosperous and successful. 9 Have I not commanded you? Be strong and courageous. Do not be afraid; do not be discouraged, for the Lord your God will be with you wherever you go."

When I look at this passage I see several values that, when applied, will help with the process of developing a healthier life. I've applied them to my own life to great effect.

The first is this, vision. Seeing what God wants to do in you, with you, through you, and for you. Secondly, courage. Being brave enough to admit you need help and seeking help both from God and his church. Thirdly, strength. Recognising that all strength for life and godliness comes from the trinity. I also believe obedience is a key value - applying the word of God to our lives in a life-giving way. The fifth value that comes to light in the passage is discipline. Consistently performing life-changing habits will bring life-changing results. Finally, endurance. Keep going, it's always too soon to quit.

God begins by giving Joshua a vision of his future. He then encourages him, on more than one occasion, to be strong and courageous. He then reminds him to obey the law, which is quickly followed with an encouragement to remain focused and consistent while meditating on his words day and night. Finally, he makes a promise to be with him wherever he goes, encouraging him to keep going regardless.

Obviously, at the heart of this passage, we see the faith of Joshua come to life. He had to believe God had a preferred future for him and the Israelites. His faith was the fuel for their journey.

I wonder, have you ever stopped to genuinely question what you believe about your salvation, do you believe that you are saved and, if so, are you prepared to do what it takes to live saved? Are you really prepared to trust the Lord your God with all your heart, leaning not on your own understanding, and in all your ways acknowledging him so that he can light your path? (Proverbs 3:5-6) Are you prepared to make God's primary rule your primary goal? Are you prepared to love the Lord your God with all your heart and with all your soul and with all your strength and with all your mind and to love your neighbours as ourselves? (Luke 10:27)

CHAPTER SEVEN

I AM HIS

It is our obedience to God which demonstrates our union with him...

"But to all who believed him and accepted him, he gave the right to become children of God"
John 1:12 NIV

For the best part of 40 years, I've supported Chelsea FC, the famous London football club. My uncle Raymond was a huge fan and his influence led me to become a follower. I've watched them gain promotion to the top tier of British football and take their place as one of the finest European soccer teams. One of the greatest sporting moments of my life was when they reached the pinnacle of English football by winning the Premier League for the first time under the management of José Mourinho, 'the special one'. José is a flamboyant, eccentric, and successful football manager, who was celebrated as the saviour of the club. During his time in charge, the club won multiple trophies and he established himself as the most successful manager in the club's history.

Much to my surprise, after a poor run of results, José's position at the club was terminated. I was devastated, not only at hearing the news of his parting but also at recognising that the values of the club had changed significantly. It had become a club like every other club that had lost its culture of honour. Our greatest manager was shown no mercy and was gone. The lack of grace in the way his dismissal was handled led me to stop wearing the club colours. I could no longer align myself with the values of the club.

The marks that we carry reveal our association with a person, place or thing. As a Christ-follower, I want the world to know that I belong to him, by observing my attitudes, my actions, my responses and my expectations. Let's face it, we all know someone who talks the talk but doesn't walk the walk. I don't want to be that guy.

The Passion Translation of Ephesians 1:11-13 states that "Through our union with Christ we too have been claimed by God as his own inheritance. Before we were even born, he gave us our destiny; that we would fulfill the plan of God who always accomplishes every purpose and plan in his heart. God's purpose was that we Jews, who were the first to long for the messianic hope, would be the first to believe in the Anointed One and bring great praise and glory to God! And because of him, when you who are not Jews heard the revelation of truth, you believed in the wonderful news of salvation. Now we have been stamped with the seal of the promised Holy Spirit."

On my office desk, I have a stamp that has the Omagh Community Church logo on it. I frequently use it to stamp stickers, that I place on items of equipment that belong to the church. It's a funny process because I know who the items belong to, but the stamp tells the world who the owner is. Here's the thing: it's not enough for us to know that we are his, the world must know too. Our values are the stamp that communicates to the world who we belong to. Jesus is quoted in John 13:35 as saying "By this everyone will know that you are my disciples if you love one another." Our values show our connection to him.

In 1 John 2:3-6, we read: "We know that we have come to know him if we keep his commands. Whoever says, "I know him," but does not do what he commands is a liar, and the truth is not in that person. But if anyone obeys his word, love for God is truly made complete in them. This is how we know we are in him: Whoever claims to live in him must live as Jesus did."

It is our obedience to God which demonstrates our union with him.

Some years ago, I was travelling on a bus across the northwest of Ireland. The back story to this story is that I love shoes, mainly white Nike trainers. The day before the journey I had purchased a stunning pair of white Nike sneakers and was wearing them for the first time that day. Picture this, I'm on the bus, minding my own business when an apparently homeless, most definitely shoeless, man gets on. As he proceeded to walk up the aisle of the bus, I heard the still, small voice of God whisper, "give him your shoes." I knew it wasn't a "would you", a request. It was a command, yet I still managed to question God. Being obedient can be difficult when it costs us something. I was very slow to act. I wrestled with God on the bus.

ME: God, are you sure?

GOD: Yes, give him your shoes.

ME: But God, I just bought them.

GOD: I know. I was there. Give him your shoes.

At this point, the man sits down on my row on the other side of the aisle.

ME: God, how on earth am I supposed to do this?

GOD: Take off the shoes and give them to him.

ME: God, are you sure?

GOD: Yes.

ME: Ok, God, I need a sign. If you don't want me to give him my brand new white Nike trainers, make the man get off at the next stop.

I looked across and at this point, the man was asleep in his seat. The conversation with God continued for what felt like an eternity until I eventually resigned myself to the fact that what he wanted was obedience, not a debate.

I'm not suggesting that you don't take time to test, wrestle with, and question God. However, if you know, and when you know, his heart, don't debate it, just do it.

As I exited the bus, I became a shoeless man. I simply placed the shoes on the sleeping man's lap and walked off.

Our obedience to God is the product of our trust in him and is lived out through our connection with the trinity.

Trust is developed through time spent in their company. Cultivating the habit of spending time with the trinity is a priority. This healthy habit cements the thought that, if I can trust God for the promise, I can trust God for the process.

Omagh Community Church is a beautiful, faith-filled, and faithful community. We have attempted to create a culture that is centred around these words spoken by God to the prophet Isaiah.

"Is not this the kind of fasting I have chosen: to loose the chains of injustice and untie the cords of the yoke, to set the oppressed free and break every yoke? Is it not to share your food with the hungry and to provide the poor wanderer with shelter— when you see the naked, to clothe them, and not to turn away from your own flesh and blood?"
Isaiah 58:6-7 NIV

We want to be a community that loves people well. We want our love for God to be demonstrated through our love for others. At our very core, we want to bring life, love, and hope to the heart of the world. Our vision determines our values and our values define our culture. When we gather together we hope that we could be instantly recognised as people who belong to God.

When someone meets you for the first time, what's the first thing they will notice about you?

I met Jennie in a nightclub in Dublin City Centre. The first thing I saw was her ankles, then her legs. I followed those legs until the opportunity for an introduction presented itself. Don't ever let anyone tell you that first impressions don't count. They do. Had it not been for those ankles and legs, the story of my life might just have been very different.

There is a lady called Eileen on the team at Omagh Community Church. Eileen is the most natural evangelist I've ever met. If you meet her, she will introduce Jesus into the conversation within the first minute. It's the first thing you'll notice about her. Her passion for Jesus is mirrored in her passion for his church. She loves to gather with people who love God.

Those who belong to God spend time with those who belong to God.

It can be easy to lose sight of the importance of being part of a faith-filled community. It can be even easier to lose the desire to be part of a faith-filled community. If we are hurting, the last place we want to be is in community. The enemy of our souls knows this too well and is always seeking to attack our desire to connect with life-giving relationships. In my darkest days, the church was the last place in the world I wanted to be.

Hebrews chapter 10 verse 10 is one of, if not my favourite verses from the bible. It tells us that "we have been made holy through the sacrifice of the body of Jesus Christ once and for all." Further on in the chapter, we can read some more foundational truths.

"Therefore, brothers and sisters, since we have confidence to enter the Most Holy Place by the blood of Jesus, by a new and living way opened for us through the curtain, that is, his body, and since we have a great priest over the house of God, let us draw near to God with a sincere heart and with the full assurance that faith brings, having our hearts sprinkled to cleanse us from a guilty conscience and having our bodies washed with pure water. Let us hold unswervingly to the hope we profess, for he who promised is faithful. And let us consider how we may spur one another on toward love and good deeds, not giving up meeting together, as some are in the habit of doing, but encouraging one another—and all the more as you see the Day approaching."
Hebrews 10:19-25 NIV

Something beautiful happens when we are in the presence of God, surrounded by God's people. We are empowered, equipped, encouraged, and released to tell the world that we are his.

I love the church. I love that I'm planted in a thriving local church. The local church is an unstoppable force, empowered by an unlimited resource, positioned as an avenue of grace connecting people to the foot of the cross, to Jesus Christ, and to the heart of the Father. It is limitless in potential, abounding in love, and God's vehicle of service to the world.

Genesis chapter 28 shows us that the church is the house of God in which people can stop, rest, dream, be ministered to by angels, hear from God, receive promises from God, and be comforted by God. The church is a place and a space for people to feel safe, belong, and encounter God. The church is a great place to build trust in God and with God.

Those who belong to God learn to trust God.

Jennie and I have got very different driving habits. This has a way of creating tension on longer car journeys, especially when I am the one driving. When Jennie is driving, she likes to use the cruise control function. I don't. I don't trust it. I don't trust it because I haven't taken the time to familiarise myself with it. I prefer being in control of the vehicle. I feel uncomfortable surrendering control to something that I don't trust. The more time we spend with a person, place, or thing, the greater the level of trust. I've never doubted a chair's ability to hold me: I sit on them all time. I've never doubted a bus driver's ability to get me where I want to go. I'm always confident in their credentials and abilities. Thankfully, I've never been in a bus accident.

Building trust can be difficult. Trust is difficult to get and easy to lose. We all have people that have broken our trust and hurt us and let us down. Maybe that's why we find it so difficult at times to trust God and surrender control to him.

The Bible encourages us in the Book of Proverbs to "trust in the Lord with all your heart and lean not on your own understanding; in all your ways submit to him, and he will make your paths straight" (Proverbs 3:5-6). The more time I spend with God, the greater level of understanding I have of his great love. He's never lied to me, left me, hurt me, forsaken me, or let me down. God can be trusted and should be trusted.

The main theme of this book is that we can trust God. The subtitle could be: "Imagine how your life would look if you were to trust God." Think about that! What would your life look like if you were to trust everything that the Bible says about God, about you, and about how we can co-exist?

I love how questions invite us to become explorers. Questions allow us to explore what we think we know. Jesus was great at asking questions that allowed his disciples to experience the joy of searching for their core beliefs. He knew the answer before asking the question but understood the process they needed to go through to change or cement their beliefs. When he asked them "who do people say that I am ?" he already knew the answer. When he asked them "who do you say that I am ?" he already knew the answer.

I love how Jesus is constantly inviting us into more of what he won for us on the cross. He is constantly inviting us to experience new levels of intimacy and greater levels of revelation.

If I believe what God says about himself, it's only a small step to believing what he says about me.

If I can place my trust in him, then I can place my trust in his words, his words that are written and also living.

If I truly believe that I am his, my life will reflect that I am his.

What would that look like for you ?

CHAPTER EIGHT

I AM CHOSEN

God's greatest desire is that you would know him as intimately as he knows you and love him as deeply as he loves you...

"Even before he made the world, God loved us and chose us in Christ to be holy and without fault in his eyes". Ephesians 1:4 NLT

I'm a huge sports fan. For as long as I can remember I've watched the Olympic Games on TV. There was a time in my life when I dreamed of winning an Olympic medal in the 800m on the athletics track. A series of poor life choices, substance misuse, and periods of homelessness took that dream away.

In the build-up to the opening ceremony of the London 2012 Olympic Games, I was presented with the fantastic opportunity of being a Torchbearer as part of the Olympic Torch Relay. I was one of 8000 people. We were the Future Flamers. I was recognised as an inspirational person in my local area due to the volunteer work with children and young people that I had been doing and was invited onto the team.

At the time, I was working alongside two missionaries, Robert and Raquel Suarez. They had travelled from America to work in Northern Ireland and became part of our church team. When they asked for my permission to nominate me, I thought nothing of it and genuinely did not expect being selected. You can imagine my surprise when I received the invitation. An invitation to take part in the greatest show on earth is a truly wonderful thing.

I was invited to participate, I had been selected, and I had been chosen in recognition of the person I had become and the work I had done.

I'm sure there were times when you received an invitation to an event, or were selected for a team and it made you feel fantastic. When we receive recognition for what we have done and it positions us in places and spaces that we've dreamed about or desired it makes us feel good.

I bet there have also been times in your life when you have been excluded. You didn't receive the invitation. You weren't selected for the team. Those were devastating moments. Maybe it was perceived that you had the wrong postcode, social status, physical appearance, skill set, or natural aptitude. Maybe circumstances beyond your control or some poor lifestyle choices left you on the outside looking in.

For a large portion of my life, I really struggled to feel part of anything. I've often struggled to see myself as a person of value and struggled to fit in. Season after season I struggled to find a place to belong and believed that past mistakes, perceived failures, self-perceived limitations, fears, and anxieties automatically disqualified me from finding and investing in life-giving relationships and experiences. I had made the mistake of believing the lie that our value is found in what we do and as a result, lived my life attempting to prove myself at every opportunity.

Living my life in that way was emotionally, physically, relationally, mentally, financially, and spiritually exhausting. If you've ever found yourself in a similar position you will appreciate the level of unrest a person can experience when carrying the excess baggage.

Feeling the need to perform in every environment to be accepted is exhausting and can only lead to burnout. It's a restless lifestyle that has the potential to cause great harm to both ourselves and our spheres of influence if we have an unhealthy sense of who we are and what we think about ourselves. Restlessness leads to weariness, weariness leads to brokenness, brokenness leads to sin and as the apostle, Paul reminds us in his letter to the church in Rome, "the wages of sin is death".

When we look at ourselves through the lens of the bible I find it helpful to remember that the kingdom of God is an upside-down kingdom with a back-to-front economy where rest is a state of mind, not a state of doing or being. Jesus invites us to find our rest in him, a rest he so magnificently secured for us on the cross, but it's an active rest, not a passive state. His invitation to enter into rest with him is an opportunity for us to walk with him, to work with him, and to watch how he does things, and, in doing so, he reminds us that everything we need for life and godliness is found in him and released through our relationship with him.

In his letter to the church in Ephesus, Paul reminds us of everything that has been made available to us because of Jesus' life, death, resurrection, and ascension. He reminds us that we have every spiritual blessing when we are united with Christ and in the right relationship with him. In other words, when we confess with our mouths that Jesus is lord and we believe in our hearts that God raised him from the dead we are saved, and as a result of this saving grace, we are in the right relationship with the trinity and in a position to live, love, serve and grow like Jesus.

In Ephesians 1:4 Paul tells us that he (God) chose us in him (Christ) before the creation of the world to be holy and blameless in his sight.

I'm reminded, comforted, and encouraged by these words, knowing that I am Chosen. I'm humbled by the realisation that my selection has nothing to do with me, what I've done or haven't done, said or didn't say, who I may or may not think I am, my postcode, my cultural background, or my heritage.

God's decision to choose me, or to choose us, has nothing to do with our conduct and everything to do with his character. It's not our emotions, our appearance, our aptitude, our financial status, our dress code, or our geographical location. It's not our confidence or courage, our successes or failures, our age, our fitness levels, our knowledge, our gender or social status, and not through physical birth. Before he spoke the world into existence God had already decided to make us, save us, partner with us, and empower us.

The courage to begin writing this book was found in a space that I created at home. I call it The Shack. It's a gym, office, and recreational space I built at the top of my garden. It presents a wonderful opportunity for me to work, train and relax in the presence of God from the comfort of my own home. The creation of this space was incredibly haphazard. When building, I didn't work to a plan, and to use an Irish term, I totally "winged it". Despite that, it turned out better than I could have expected and I'm extremely pleased with the outcome.

The biblical narrative of the creation story, the outworking of the commencement of God's plan for humanity, tells us that God spoke the world into existence and that everything he made was good to him. Everything God made pleased him. God makes good things and he makes a specific design not in the haphazard winging-it style that I'm all too familiar with.

It's no accident therefore that Paul writes these words to the Galatian church "But even before I was born, God chose me and called me by his marvellous grace. Then it pleased him"
Galatians 1:15 NLT

The following words are attributed to George McDonald: "I would rather be what God chose to make than the most glorious creature that I could think of; for to have been thought about, born in God's thought, and then made by God, is the dearest, grandest, and most precious thing in all thinking".

I wonder when was the last time you stopped to think about the fact that when God chose to make you it pleased him. Not only did it please him, but it also continues to please him. You didn't just happen, you were created with passion for a purpose. God in his divinity does not regret creating you in your humanity and despite everything you have done, everything you will do, and the fact he knows everything about you, he still chose to make you. Your past, present or future were not a deterrent to the creator of the universe when it came to the choice of making you.

When speaking to the prophet Jeremiah, God said this "Before I formed you in the womb I knew you, before you were born I set you apart; I appointed you as a prophet to the nations."
Jeremiah 1:5 NIV

This conversation comes at the beginning of Jeremiah's ministry. Jeremiah was appointed by God to speak to his people. God's desire for his people was that they would become aware of their behaviour, that they might understand their rebellious behaviour, immoral principles and unusual worship practices would not escape his judgement.

After a glance at the life of Jeremiah, you would be forgiven for thinking that Jeremiah significantly failed in his mission, essentially he failed to convince those in his sphere of influence not to rebel against Babylon, he failed to save Jerusalem from destruction and is best remembered as the weeping prophet who mourns that destruction.

I take great comfort in knowing that no other prophet that we find in the bible had a more intimate or passionate relationship with God than Jeremiah. Despite our human perception of failure and success, God was pleased with

Jeremiah. I'm greatly encouraged in knowing that God was more interested in intimacy with Jeremiah than the impact of Jeremiah. It simply boils down to this, God is more interested in our faith in him than our feats for him.

I believe with all of my heart that God's greatest desire is that you would know him as intimately as he knows you and love him as deeply as he loves you, that his primary will in choosing to make you was to enjoy a relationship with you that isn't centred on your conduct, that isn't dependent on your output but rather dependent on his input.

Intimacy with God the Father is the birthright of every person who has received new life in Jesus Christ and is sustained through the person, power, and presence of the Holy Spirit.

I've said it before but I'll repeat it, there has never been a day in my life that I've not believed in God. My issue has always been that I didn't understand how deep, wide, and vast his love is and always has been for me. I could never understand why a perfect, sovereign and holy God would want to have anything to do with someone as broken as me.

My wife and I have both been in the darkest of places. We met each other amid our brokenness and carried that brokenness into each other's lives and the lives of our children. When I first met Jennie, after admiring her legs I bought drugs from her, went to her flat in the centre of Dublin, and never left. Some people describe their relationship as a whirlwind romance. I'd describe ours as a tornado of torment that included lots of substance abuse, affairs, theft, grief, mistrust, suicide attempts, grief, anger, and bitterness that combined led to the breakdown of our relationship and a long period of separation.

My Jesus journey began after Jennie extended an invitation to attend a church event that she was speaking at while we were still separated.

Jennie didn't carry the same religious baggage as me and found faith in Jesus before me. When she said yes to Jesus' invitation to follow him, the transformation process began and who she was becoming was so much brighter than the darkness of who she had been. The absent mother became present, the broken drug dealer became an award-winning student on her journey toward becoming an exceptional midwife. The significant thing about her was her understanding of Jesus, full of grace of truth.

Until the day I die, I pray I never forget the moment Jesus used Jennie to get my attention to demonstrate his grace and truth. Equally significant was the response of Andrew Mc Court who leads a thriving community at Bayside Church. Andrew welcomed me with open arms into the church, lead me through a disciple journey that has very much influenced the husband, father and leader that I am today.

Up until this point, I misunderstood the character of God and believed deep in my heart that he was sitting on his throne in the heavens above waiting to poke me with his holy pitchfork at the first opportunity he got. I certainly feared God but had never managed to progress to the relationship made available through the cross of Jesus Christ. When Jennie shared her story in that church on that very special day I caught a glimpse of the grace of God. I knew what Jennie was like before she found faith and could see who she had become. She attributed that change to the grace of God and I thought if God can do that for her then surely he could do it for me.

The gap between my humanity and the divinity of The Trinity had been closed and my relationship with them was restored.

When writing to the early church, the apostle James encourages us to "draw near to god and he will draw near to you" (James 4:8). He reminds us that God chooses to be with those who choose to be with him, that pursuing intimacy with god as his children leads to greater levels of intimacy with him as our father. He closes the gap between us when we choose to follow him. When we choose to be with him, to accept his invitation to spend eternity with him, he takes up residence inside of us and promises never to reject us, leave us or forsake us.

The fact that the sovereign lord has chosen to spend eternity with me never ceases to amaze me. I have to wrestle with this thought regularly. God in his divinity decided before the world began that despite my broken humanity, he would like to spend eternity with me and extends that invitation to you too.

When putting this chapter together I thought it would be fun to ask some people how they would describe me using only one word. Some of the responses were; luminous, genuine, captivating, exuberant, gregarious, authentic, audacious, caring, exhorter, and faithful.

It's funny that we rarely see ourselves in the same way that those around us do. If I was to describe myself I may say that I'm over-enthusiastic. My enthusiasm for life can be a beautiful thing but I appreciate it also being exhausting to be around.

I think it's fair to say that we each have a misplaced sense of identity that has been shaped by the environments, expectations, and experiences of our past. Like seriously, let's face it, I can't imagine anyone wanting to be with me all the time for all of the time because in my head more often than not I feel like I'm hard work for others. Thankfully, God doesn't look at us in the same way we look at ourselves and views us through the lens of heaven from his throne of grace which in turn means that there is nothing, including our misplaced sense of identity and our multifaceted and diverse personalities that can separate us from the love of God found in Christ Jesus making us children of God.

In this letter to the church in Rome, the apostle Paul writes "And I am convinced that nothing can ever separate us from God's love. Neither death nor life, neither angels nor demons, neither our fears for today nor our worries about tomorrow—not even the powers of hell can separate us from God's love. No power in the sky above or in the earth below—indeed, nothing in all creation will ever be able to

separate us from the love of God that is revealed in Christ Jesus our Lord"
Romans 8: 38-39 NIV

It's an undeniable and unbreakable truth that God's desire to have intimacy with his children transcends both time and logic and nothing will or could stand in his way.

The enemy of your soul would love nothing more than to rob you of these truths, he knows that in doing so he can attack your sense of value. He will attempt to rob you of your sense of identity and try to make you question the very purpose of your existence here on earth. He is described as a thief who comes to steal, kill and destroy. If he can steal your identity, he can kill your purpose and destroy your impact.

The good news for us today is that we can say with confidence as individuals who collectively make up the family of God, "I AM CHOSEN".

Recognising that God chose to make you, save you, send you and spend eternity with you simply means this, you can move to new levels of intimacy with him, stop striving for his approval and rest in his love.

CHAPTER NINE

I AM GIFTED

God is a great gift-giver. His generosity is unrivalled...

"His divine power has given us everything we need for a godly life through our knowledge of him who called us by his own glory and goodness." 2 Peter 1:3 NIV

Christian Churches Ireland runs a leadership training school called CCI Academy. During a recent Academy module held in Discovery Church in Galway, I was hosted by Daniel and Tharangi Jayakumar. I was blessed with their company and the company of their beautiful children. Daniel and Tharangi are two former Academy students and are also two of the most generous people I've ever met. From the moment I entered their home until the moment I left, the generosity I experienced was quite overwhelming, in the best possible way. I'm not exaggerating when I say that every fifteen minutes Daniel had something to give me. This wonderful man even offered to cook sea bass for me when it was nearly midnight. These guys are as generous with their words as they are with their home and their contents. I went to bed with a full stomach and an even fuller heart. These guys were abundant in their giving and went over and above in ensuring that I felt welcome, loved, and appreciated. To top it all off, Daniel gave me the shirt off his back as I was leaving. I've never experienced or even witnessed this type of lavish generosity outside a kingdom-focused community.

Paul writes in Ephesians 1:7 -9 (NIV) "In him we have redemption through his blood, the forgiveness of sins, in accordance with the riches of God's grace that he lavished on us. With all wisdom and understanding, he made known to us the mystery of his will according to his good pleasure, which he purposed in Christ."

When I think about the word "lavished" I think of overwhelming generosity, an abundance of giving, the type of over-and-above gifting that rarely makes sense. Paul reminds us that God's gift of grace is given freely, generously, and abundantly in a way that doesn't make sense. He reminds us that with all his wisdom and knowledge he has entrusted us with his abundant grace.

In choosing to make us, save us, adopt us, forgive us and gift us, God has made us stewards of his grace.

I have an awful habit of losing things. I would go so far as to say that I am lethal when it comes to looking after important things. My family will tell you that I am notorious for losing my car keys and that every morning there is a blind panic before the school run. I have this annoying habit of thinking it's a really good idea to leave things in safe places. It turns out that leaving things in safe places is never a good idea. You name it, I lose it. Passports, Driver's License, Glasses, Phones, Documents - nothing is safe in my hands. A safe place really means a lost place. Yet, God in his infinite wisdom chooses to entrust me, and you, and all of us, with his abounding grace. Not only that, but he's also gifted us in such a way that we use the gift of grace to serve those around us. He gifts us in such a way that we can add value to our spheres of influence with the superabundant grace that's working in us, through us, and for us.

In his first letter, Peter writes: "As each one has received a special gift, employ it in serving one another as good stewards of the multifaceted grace of God." 1Peter 4:10 New American Standard Bible

The guys at Omagh Community Church will tell you that I am a huge gift advocate. They may even accuse me of sounding like a broken record. I believe that we are all uniquely gifted and when we each operate in the area of our gift we come alive and thrive. Having spent most of my life feeling useless I feel deeply impassioned that everyone should know that they are gifted.

Gary Rucci is the Lead Pastor at Rivercity Family Church, Brisbane. Several years ago, he visited Cornerstone City Church, Derry. He spoke to us about what many people describe as the motivational gifts of God and led us through Romans chapter 12 verses six to eight.

"We have different gifts, according to the grace given to each of us. If your gift is prophesying, then prophesy in accordance with your faith; if it is serving, then serve; if it is teaching, then teach; if it is to encourage, then give encouragement; if it is giving, then give generously; if it is to lead, do it diligently; if it is to show mercy, do it cheerfully."
Romans 12:6-8

Up until this point I had never understood why certain people seem best suited to certain environments while others look like fish out of water. There is a possibility that at some point in your life, you've encountered a teacher that you just know wasn't best suited to teaching or a nurse that made you feel like the most important person that ever lived. Understanding what motivates and drives us is vitally important when it comes to positioning ourselves as stewards of God's grace. I believe that when God was knitting us together in our mother's womb he gifted us in such a way that not only would we thrive but also that those around us would be encouraged to thrive through our gift too. It's no accident that my wife is an outstanding midwife: she has an incredibly strong mercy gift. She was destined to find a role that would allow her to love people well.

I've spent most of my life being a really strong starter and a terrible finisher. I've had more jobs in more industries than any man should have in two lifetimes, let alone one. I've sold insurance, worked in retail, studied a variety of subjects, fixed phones, and laboured on building sites. None of these jobs were what I was born to do. I'm a natural encourager. I come alive in environments and relationships that allow me to encourage. I was born with the gift of encouragement. God created me to be a cheerleader. The freedom that comes from knowing this is immeasurable and no doubt has added great value to my sphere of influence. Who doesn't need a cheerleader?

I've met so many people who have either been written off by the world or have written themselves off because they don't believe, or no one has told them, that they have something to offer.

In 2020 Chris Nikic became the first athlete with Down syndrome to complete an IRONMAN triathlon: a 2.4-mile swim followed by a 112-mile bicycle ride, ending with a 26.2-mile marathon. In Britain, 90% of babies diagnosed with Down Syndrome are aborted before birth according to the National Down Syndrome Cytogenic Register. That means that in essence 90% of those babies are written off while God is knitting them together in their mother's womb.

If you visit @chrisnikic on Instagram you will see the following words in his bio. "I want to honour God and inspire others like me". Chris and his family have embraced the idea that we are all gifted and they seek to inform others in their sphere of influence that they are gifted too.

The good news for you today is that although the world might have written you off, God hasn't.

The Old Testament book of Judges describes a life-changing encounter that Gideon experienced with the Angel of the Lord after Gideon had written himself off.

"The angel of the Lord came and sat down under the oak in Ophrah that belonged to Joash the Abiezrite, where his son Gideon was threshing wheat in a winepress to keep it from the Midianites. When the angel of the Lord appeared to Gideon, he said, "The Lord is with you, mighty warrior." "Pardon me, my lord," Gideon replied, "but if the Lord is with us, why has all this happened to us? Where are all his wonders that our ancestors told us about when they said, 'Did not the Lord bring us up out of Egypt?' But now the Lord has abandoned us and given us into the hand of Midian." The Lord turned to him and said, "Go in the

strength you have and save Israel out of Midian's hand. Am I not sending you?" "Pardon me, my lord," Gideon replied, "but how can I save Israel? My clan is the weakest in Manasseh, and I am the least in my family."
Judges 6:11-15 NIV

Gideon had written himself off. He couldn't see beyond his current circumstances and was massively influenced by his environment. He couldn't see what God could see.

You might have written yourself off. God hasn't. God calls things as though they are. When he speaks, it's as if it's already done.

Jennie and I became the lead Pastors of Omagh Community Church back in October 2013. We were inexperienced, naive, and nervous but above all committed. My good friend, mentor, and leader, Pastor Gary Davidson, pioneer and former national leader of Assemblies of God Ireland, gave us one of the best pieces of advice I've ever received just before we started in our new roles. He said, "No matter what happens, even when you don't feel like it, even when you think you have nothing to say or nothing to offer, just keep turning up. God can't work through you to lead your people if you are not in the room."

I've lost count of the number of times I've written myself off since Gary shared those great words of wisdom with me. I've lost count of the number of times I've felt completely disillusioned. I've lost count of the number of setbacks I've encountered. I've lost count of the number of times I've felt like quitting. I've lost count of the number of times I've allowed my feelings to fool me and derail any forward momentum that I've been experiencing.

Before we started on our great adventure in Omagh, we also received some equally insightful advice from Pastor Brian Somerville. He said, "Know your calling. Your calling will sustain you."

In moments of doubt, denial, and disillusionment, our anchor has been our calling. Through the betrayal, the brokenness, and the burnout, our anchor has been our calling. God had given us a very simple yet definitive message to share with the world.

YOUR FUTURE IS BRIGHTER THAN THE DARKNESS OF YOUR PAST.

When I decided to get healthier, I dared myself to believe everything that God had said about me and written for me. I realised that my feelings might fool me but that my faith would fuel me. I decided that even if I felt like hiding or giving up, or if I became disillusioned or ran into a wall of doubt, what God says about me would be the defining factor in anything that I would say or do. The very fact that I am writing this book, and that you are now reading it, is a testament to the benefits of such a way of thinking. I've always felt like I had something to say but I never dared to say it. I allowed my feelings to fool me because I never actually believed that I am gifted.

In his Gospel, Matthew reminds us that we are here to be light, bringing out the God colours in the world. He is quoting Jesus and tells us that God is not a secret to be kept. We are told that he has made us light-bearers and that we shouldn't be hidden under a bucket.

We can apply these verses to our own lives and our giftedness. God has designed us to make a difference, gifted us with the ability to make a difference, and put us in places where we can make a difference. You are gifted. I am gifted. We are gifted.

Our God is a great gift-giver. His generosity is unrivalled.

When describing God's generous gifting, James puts it like this "So, my very dear friends, don't get thrown off course. Every desirable and beneficial gift comes out of heaven. The gifts are rivers of light cascading down from the Father of Light. There is nothing deceitful in God, nothing two-faced, nothing fickle. He brought us to life using the true Word, showing us off as the crown of all his creatures."
James 1:16-18 MSG

Henry Richard Enfield is an English comedian, actor, writer, and director. He is best known for his work on British TV. One of his many fictional characters is Tim, Nice but Dim, who represents an old colloquial expression that describes a good-natured person who is also rather unintelligent - not exactly the brightest of sparks. I feel like the enemy of our souls has tricked us into thinking that we are a bit dim, that our light can't or won't shine brightly, that we have nothing to offer, and that our giftedness is limited, or at worst non-existent.

God has called us to rise and shine. His glory is upon us. He promises that nations will come to see the light he has given us and that mighty kings will come to see its radiance. He commands us to look up and live in community. He promises that if we do, we will look radiant, our hearts will throb with joy and we will receive an abundant blessing. Lavish generosity will be shown to us.

The good news is this, "His divine power has given us everything we need for a godly life through our knowledge of him who called us by his own glory and goodness."
2 Peter 1:3

CHAPTER TEN

I AM ENOUGH

Perfect is perfect. Perfect isn't more. Perfect isn't less. Perfect is just perfect...

"Praise be to the God and Father of our Lord Jesus Christ, who has blessed us in the heavenly realms with every spiritual blessing in Christ."
Ephesians 1:3 NIV

I've met a lot of great characters throughout my life. One such person was the effervescent Dr. Michael ffrench-O'Carroll. He was a prominent Irish politician and medical doctor who, in his later years, had a special interest in addiction and the treatment of addiction. I first met him in Cuan Mhuire, Athy. I was the first person to successfully complete their thirteen-week residential detox program which he oversaw.

During my first encounter with this larger-than-life personality, he tried to encourage me by telling me that I was "more than enough". I was very broken at the time and, instead of finding encouragement in these words, I felt that they represented the unrealistic expectations associated with a standard I could never reach. At this point in my life, my inner voice and my inner critic were the loudest they'd ever been. I remember sitting in the waiting room for that first encounter and thinking to myself, "how on earth did I end up here?". I had started as a grade-A student, a successful athlete, a keen musician, and a singer. But now I had become separated from my family, I had lost contact with my daughter, I couldn't return to my home, and I had just endured another period of homelessness. The thought of being "more than enough" was quite simply inconceivable. Even thinking that I was "enough" at that stage of my life was a stretch too far.

There is no doubting the power of the spoken and written word. Words have power. Words can either make us or break us. Proverbs 15:4 teaches us: "Gentle words bring life and health; a deceitful tongue crushes the spirit."

After hearing these words from the doctor, I began to live with a false sense of expectation. Since the doctor had said that I was more than enough then I felt that I needed to be more than enough. But always trying to be more than enough was the very thing that led me to burnout. When people use the language of "more than enough", it's easy to be sucked into a cycle of over-working, over-performing and over-achieving. For someone with a low sense of self, the idea of becoming more than enough has the potential to have a very negative impact.

The same can be said for someone with a heightened sense of self. Thinking too much of ourselves also has the potential to impact us negatively. If you feel like you are more than enough, you run the risk of feeling like you don't need anything or anyone. You can miss growth opportunities. You can be unaware of your blind spots. The thought of needing a saviour might also be a stretch too far.

I've decided not to try to be more than enough. I've also decided that I'm going to believe that I AM ENOUGH.

My absolute favourite verse in all of the bible is Hebrews 10:14. I love the whole chapter. Understanding it and applying it to my life has helped to bring changes that I am enjoying in the season I find myself in. It states that "For by one sacrifice he has made perfect forever those who are being made holy".

Perfect is perfect. Perfect isn't more. Perfect isn't less. Perfect is just perfect. Perfect means having the required or desirable elements, qualities, or characteristics. Being perfect means for it to be as good as it is possible to be. Right now at this moment, I AM ENOUGH. Right now at this moment as a child of God, you too are enough. We are perfect and we are being made holy. We are enough and yet there is still more to come.

I'm not sure how that makes you feel. I want to tell you how it makes me feel. It makes me feel free. It's the most freeing thought I have ever had. The ability to wake up in the morning knowing that I am enough has had a dramatic impact on my life. Any sense of fear connected to my sense of lack has disappeared and the voice of the enemy has been silenced. Having the capacity to walk into a room and know that I carry value into that room is the best feeling in the world.

Paul writes in Ephesians 1:3, "Praise be to the God and Father of our Lord Jesus Christ, who has blessed us in the heavenly realms with every spiritual blessing in Christ."

The word "every" is another brilliant word. It's typically used before a singular noun to refer to all the individual members of a set without exception. It's another perfect word. As children of God, that means right now we have the perfect amount of everything we need to live the life

Jesus died for us to have. Simply put, we are enough and we have enough.

In his second letter, Peter writes these words, "By his divine power, God has given us everything we need for living a godly life. We have received all of this by coming to know him, the one who called us to himself by means of his marvellous glory and excellence."
2 Peter 1:3 NLT

The challenge for us is two-fold. Firstly, can I believe that Jesus is who he says he is, and secondly, can I believe what he says about me? It's the premise of the book. Imagine. Imagine what your life would look like if you were to believe everything God has said about you and written for you.

Before we begin to imagine ourselves believing what God has said about us and written for us, I feel we should ask ourselves what we truly believe about God. If we can believe that God is who he says he is, then the logical progression should be that we can believe what he says about us.

In the opening part of his letter to the church in Colossae, Paul uses these words to describe Jesus:

"The Son is the image of the invisible God, the firstborn over all creation. For in him all things were created: things in heaven and on earth, visible and invisible, whether thrones or powers or rulers or authorities; all things have been created through him and for him. He is before all

things, and in him all things hold together. And he is the head of the body, the church; he is the beginning and the firstborn from among the dead, so that in everything he might have the supremacy. For God was pleased to have all his fullness dwell in him, and through him to reconcile to himself all things, whether things on earth or things in heaven, by making peace through his blood, shed on the cross."
Colossians 1:15-20

The greatest question we will ever have to answer is this: Who is Jesus and what do I believe about him?

It's good to realise that God is not surprised by our questions. I touched on this very topic in a previous chapter. Asking questions is a great thing. Without questions, there are no answers. We need answers to understand what we believe to be true. Jesus often asked his disciples questions. It's worth remembering that every time he asked a question, he already knew the answer. The questions weren't for his benefit, they were for the benefit of the person searching for the answer.

I love reading about the exchange between Jesus and his disciples that Matthew describes in his Gospel:

"When Jesus came to the region of Caesarea Philippi, he asked his disciples, "Who do people say the Son of Man is?" They replied, "Some say John the Baptist; others say Elijah; and still others, Jeremiah or one of the prophets." "But what about you?" he asked. "Who do you say I am?" Simon Peter answered, "You are the Messiah, the Son of

the living God." Jesus replied, "Blessed are you, Simon son of Jonah, for this was not revealed to you by flesh and blood, but by my Father in heaven. And I tell you that you are Peter, and on this rock, I will build my church, and the gates of Hades will not overcome it. I will give you the keys of the kingdom of heaven; whatever you bind on earth will be bound in heaven, and whatever you loose on earth will be loosed in heaven." Then he ordered his disciples not to tell anyone that he was the Messiah."
Matthew 16:13-20 NIV

Imagine being a first-century Christian and encountering the visible image of the invisible God. Imagine being Peter at that moment and recognising Jesus for who he is. Imagine the impact of that on his life, or on your life: the fullness of God before you; his divinity embracing you; touching the Word who became flesh; eternity breathing on you; the way maker, the miracle worker, the promise keeper, staring you in the face; the alpha and omega, the beginning and the end, in physical form, walking the earth with you. Imagine that: the human face of God with you and inviting you to follow him; the human face of God calling you as your good shepherd!

In Psalm 23 David writes: "The Lord is my shepherd, I lack nothing. He makes me lie down in green pastures, he leads me beside quiet waters, he refreshes my soul. He guides me along the right paths for his name's sake. Even though I walk through the darkest valley, I will fear no evil, for you are with me; your rod and your staff, they comfort me. You prepare a table before me in the presence of my enemies. You anoint my head with oil; my cup overflows. Surely

your goodness and love will follow me all the days of my life, and I will dwell in the house of the Lord forever."
Psalms 23:1-6 NIV

David is reminding us that as children of God, we are enough and we have enough. We lack nothing.

The invitation to follow Jesus is an invitation to enter his rest. The cross was enough.

The invitation to follow Jesus is an invitation to receive his provision. He has enough.

The invitation to follow Jesus is an invitation into his presence. He is enough.

The invitation to follow Jesus is an invitation to have his protection. He gives enough.

Everything you think and believe about yourself at this moment in your life has been shaped by your experiences, the environments where you've found yourself, and the expectations you and others have of you. Our lives are a product of the things we believe to be true.

For the best part of the last 15 years, I have mostly felt like a fraud. I genuinely thought I wasn't good enough to lead, love, and serve. It is the most paralysing feeling I've ever had to experience. It's rooted in the lie that "I'm not good enough". The devil is the father of lies. He is a dirty rotten stinking big fat smelly liar. But the funny thing is that if you were to meet someone on the street and they were to speak to you in the visible world in the same way that he speaks to you in the invisible world, you would find it difficult to control yourself and you would fight back. When Jesus was confronted by the devil and his lies he didn't hold back, he fought back. Jesus fought the lies of Satan with the word of God. He fought temptation with truth. **The father of lies was defeated when the word of God was activated.** I love the interaction we see taking place between Jesus and the Devil in the fourth chapter of Matthew's gospel.

"Then Jesus was led by the Spirit into the wilderness to be tempted by the devil. After fasting forty days and forty nights, he was hungry. The tempter came to him and said, "If you are the Son of God, tell these stones to become bread." Jesus answered, "It is written: 'Man shall not live on bread alone, but on every word that comes from the mouth of God.' " Then the devil took him to the holy city and had him stand on the highest point of the temple. "If you are the Son of God," he said, "throw yourself down. For it is written: 'He will command his angels concerning you, and they will lift you up in their hands, so that you will not strike your foot against a stone.' " Jesus answered him, "It is also written: 'Do not put the Lord your God to the test.'" Again, the devil took him to a very high mountain and showed him all the kingdoms of the world and their splendour. "All this I will give you," he said, "if you will bow down and worship me." Jesus said to him, "Away from me, Satan! For it is written: 'Worship the Lord your God, and serve him only.' " Then the devil left him, and angels came and attended him."
Matthew 4:1-11 NIV

To be honest, it was sometimes easier to believe the lies of the enemy. If I allow myself to believe the lies of the enemy it means I don't have to activate faith and can stay stuck. However, Jesus Christ did not endure all the suffering on his journey to the cross and then die on the cross for me to stay stuck. His death alone brought a shout from heaven that I am a person of value, that we are people of value. His public humiliation on the way to the cross tells me that I matter to God, that we matter to God. His blood that was shed on the cross tells me that we are enough.

I can't put it any better than this.

The Blood of Christ says that I AM ENOUGH.

"Every word of God is flawless; he is a shield to those who take refuge in him." Proverbs 30:5 NIV

Printed in Great Britain
by Amazon